The Hidden Self
I0753753
Mystic Mermaid.
Mystic Mermaid by Naomi

Cover Design: Bee Williamson
Front & Back Cover Artwork: Bee Williamson, Naomi Downie
Layout and Design: Bee Williamson of HIVE www.hive.id.au

Printed and Bound in Australia by BookPOD

This book is available for purchase from:
www.bookstore.bookpod.com.au
Phone: (03) 9803 4481
web: www.bookpod.com.au

For the Cataloguing-in-Publication Data
refer to the National Library of Australia

ISBN: 978-0-646-50776-7

If you'd like to contact Naomi:
naomimdownie@netscape.net
to purchase artworks:
http://www.redbubble.com/people/naomimdownie

Contact Bee at: hello@hive.id.au
to purchase artworks:
http://www.redbubble.com/people/beebop

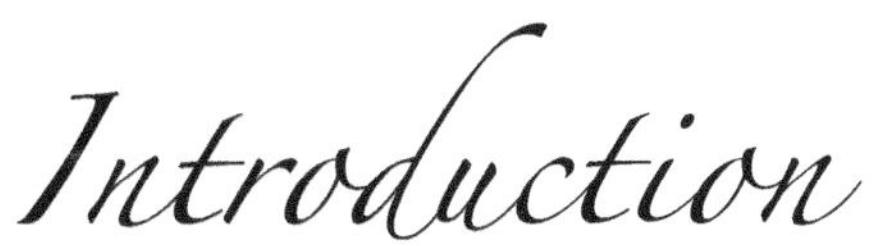

Introduction

In 2007 Bee Williamson and I met at a women writers' group, called Woman's Word. The group culminated in a published zine of our poetry and prose.

In the excitement of creating the cover for the group's book, Bee and I realised we were both artists and poets. This naturally led to a conversation about doing a project together in the near future.

During the whole of 2008 we went through the stages of dreaming together about what we wanted to give to the world, our themes, the impact of the book and the launch, then came the hard work of drawing, painting and editing years of art and poetry. The process of bringing our two collections together, finding the best design and layout, was a major learning curve, as it was the first book for both of us. We had both experienced past collaborations which had fallen through, so were determined to believe in the project, the work and the friendship.

Through emails, text messages, facebook, red bubble and long lunches and coffees across two states, we have got to know each other's shared reality and philosophy. We have discovered how we both use poetry as a way of expressing emotions and of exploring our identity, what is to be a woman and what it is to be human.

We were also touched to find both of us experienced visions and dreams as a source of channeling our creative inspiration on to paper and both of us found that nature really helped restore us after all these mystic moments into grounded truth.

Our title "The Hidden Self" comes from a time of crossroads where the project was stalling. We discovered that the fear of exposing something that had long been private was blocking our path. For me art had become something I did for myself – I had not exhibited for years - and was about deeply personal inner experiences, so to begin to put myself out there again was upsetting me. For Bee poetry was her hidden self: the secret passion for writing was just for herself and she never shared them with others. Her art also reveals a hidden dream. It is often about the joy of movement, expressing and exploring her unrequited ambition to become a contemporary dancer.

So this has become the title of our book, about honoring these Hidden Selves that long to be heard, seen and valued. It is our hope for others that "as we let our own light shine, we unconsciously give other people permission to do the same" - Nelson Mandela's speech written by Marianne Williamson. This book is gift from our heart to yours with all the wisdom, beauty and hope we have found.

By Naomi M. Downie

Art is the conversation between lovers.
Art offers an opening for the heart.
True art makes a divine silence in the soul
Break into applause.
Hafiz

Ten thousand flowers in spring
the moon in autumn,
a cool breeze in summer,
snow in winter.
If your mind isn't clouded by unnecessary things,
this is the best season of your life.
Wu-men

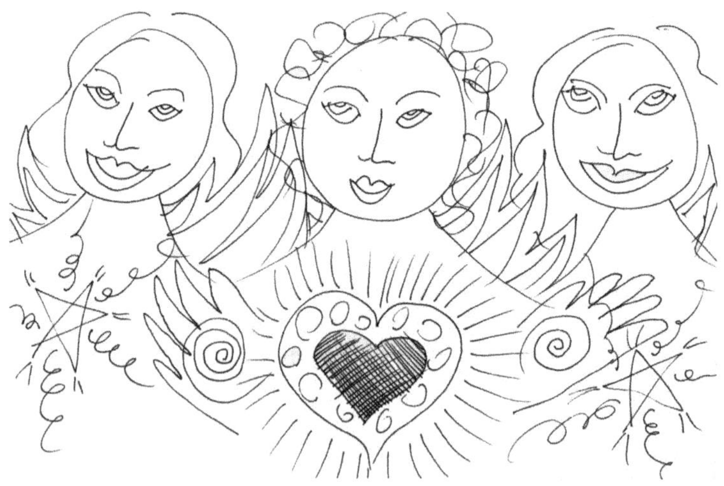

Earth Angels by Bee

Acknowledgements

BEE

A big Thank You goes to Nilgun Guven for organising "Woman's Word" and being my mentor for "Hamlet's Angel" and the "Swimming in my Head" performance. Also to Kelly- Lee Hickey for seeding this project. To Gilli Smyth for her continuing support of my spiritual development and her guidance and encouragement, bringing about the awareness of the Goddess faith and the importance of artistic originality. Gratitude to my brother Tali, who watered the seeds of inspiration and went first. Love to Michelle Leber for her continual nourishing support. Marjetka McMahon for believing in me and giving me the opportunity to participate in organising Roarhouse. To Maribel Steel for being the best friend one could ever hope to find, and her help with editing and reading. Sandra Hutchins at VCA, her belief in my work and unusual style. To Jessie Huon, her inspiration as friend and writer and support in the early days of experimentation. To Charlotte Amos for her reading, feedback and encouragement as only a true friend can. I would like to thank my mum Carol, my dad Harry and Keith for the care and support they have all shown.

NAOMI

I would like to acknowledge my mentors from Newcastle Poetry at the Pub, Bill Iden and Norman Talbot. To celebrate my comrades Andrew Shillam and Brad Evans, the first poets I ever met, their passion and love of poetry rocked my world. A big thank you to Ron Hartree, who encouraged me by providing a space to create my art. Terence Garrott, head teacher of meditation and discussion at the Newcastle School of Philosophy. To Doreen Hopkins, my Tai Chi teacher, who led me to quiet places of beauty. Mark Shering, God bless my IT man. Dad for the use of his home, computer and for his love and support. Thanks Maribel Steel for editing my work. Margaret Tuting, the first mystic I ever met - she listened deeply. Many blessings to Bruno Thiel, for being my muse and medicine. Thanks to Mum for all the art exhibitions and libraries you took me to.

Contents

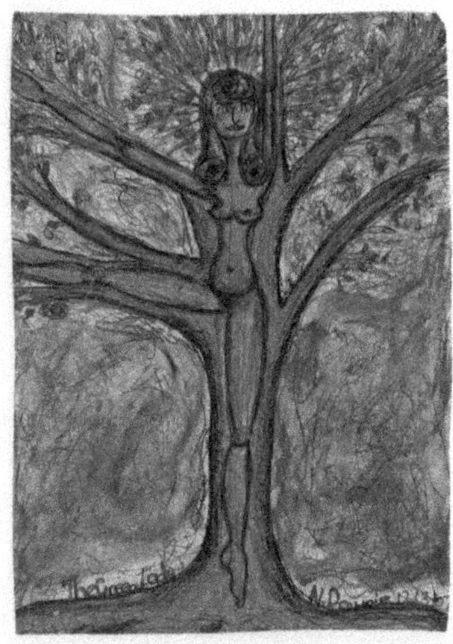

The Green Dancer by Naomi

BIOGRAPHIES

I rain

Because your meadows call

For God

I weave light into words so that

When your mind holds them

Your eyes will relinquish their sadness,

Turn bright, a little brighter, giving to us

The way a candle does

To the dark.

Hafiz

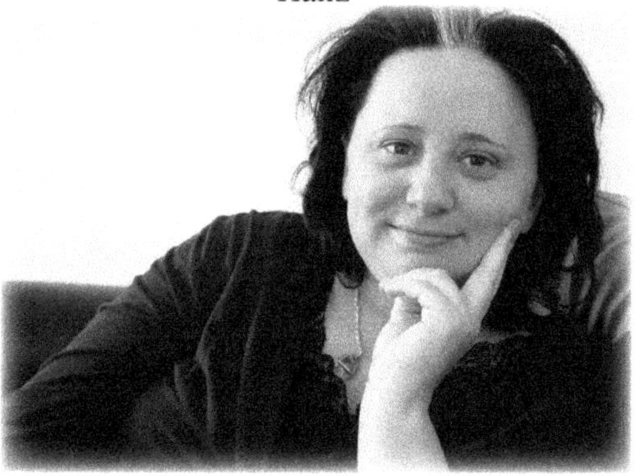

Naomi Downie studied Diploma of Art Therapy at Phoenix Institute in Melbourne and regularly gives workshops using meditation & music to inspire people to create art. She has also studied Fine Arts at Newcastle TAFE and has a Bachelor in Psychology. Naomi has been a part of group art exhibitions at Newcastle Regional Gallery, Gilbert Street Gallery and Tafe Gallery, Lovett's Gallery and Ron Hartree's studio. She has performed poetry at Peoples Performance Project 2 & 3, Dan O'Connell pub, Roarhouse at Esplanade Hotel with a harpist and at South Melbourne pub with a belly dancer and drummer. She has published her work with the Woman's Art Register bulletin, the Woman's Room net zine, Moment's zine, Woman's Word anthology and Newcastle Poetry at the Pub Anthology 2007 & 2008. Written a play and performed "No Think" with Art House Five, 1997. Part of the poetry committee organising the Multicultural Literature Night and co-editor 'Poesis' book, 1998.

BIOGRAPHIES

Out beyond ideas of wrongdoing and rightdoing,

there is a field.

I'll meet you there.

When the soul lies down in that grass,

the world is too full to talk about.

Ideas, language, even the phrase each other

doesn't make sense

Rumi

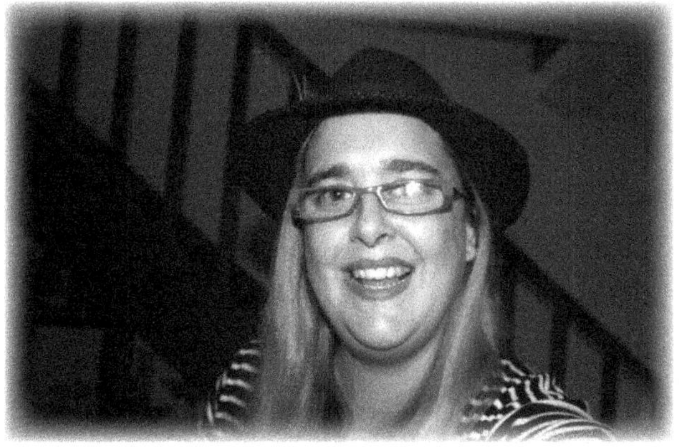

Bee comes from a family of artists - poets, painters, musicians and writers - and is passionate and committed to her many artistic expressions. She graduated from the VCA as Bachelor of Visual and Performing Arts in 1998. While still a child, Bee grew up going to The Street Poets gigs around Melbourne. She remembers all the regulars at Cafe Jammin', Middle Park. In 2006 she began organising the lineup for Roarhouse spoken word gigs. In 2007, she was involved in Woman's Word and their publication Woman's Word - New Works by Ten Women Writers, launched at the Port Melbourne Neighbourhood House. In the same year she received a Cultural Development Fund from the City of Port Phillip for a reading of her play Hamlet's Angel at the National Young Writers' Festival in Newcastle. Since 2004 she has had 12 exhibitions of artwork around galleries in Melbourne. She was also published in C.R.O.P. Harvest; People's Performance Project Bubbles of Resistance Rising: Beyond Borders and Binaries; and reviewed 'Camille - La Fille du Cirque' for Melbourne Stage online.

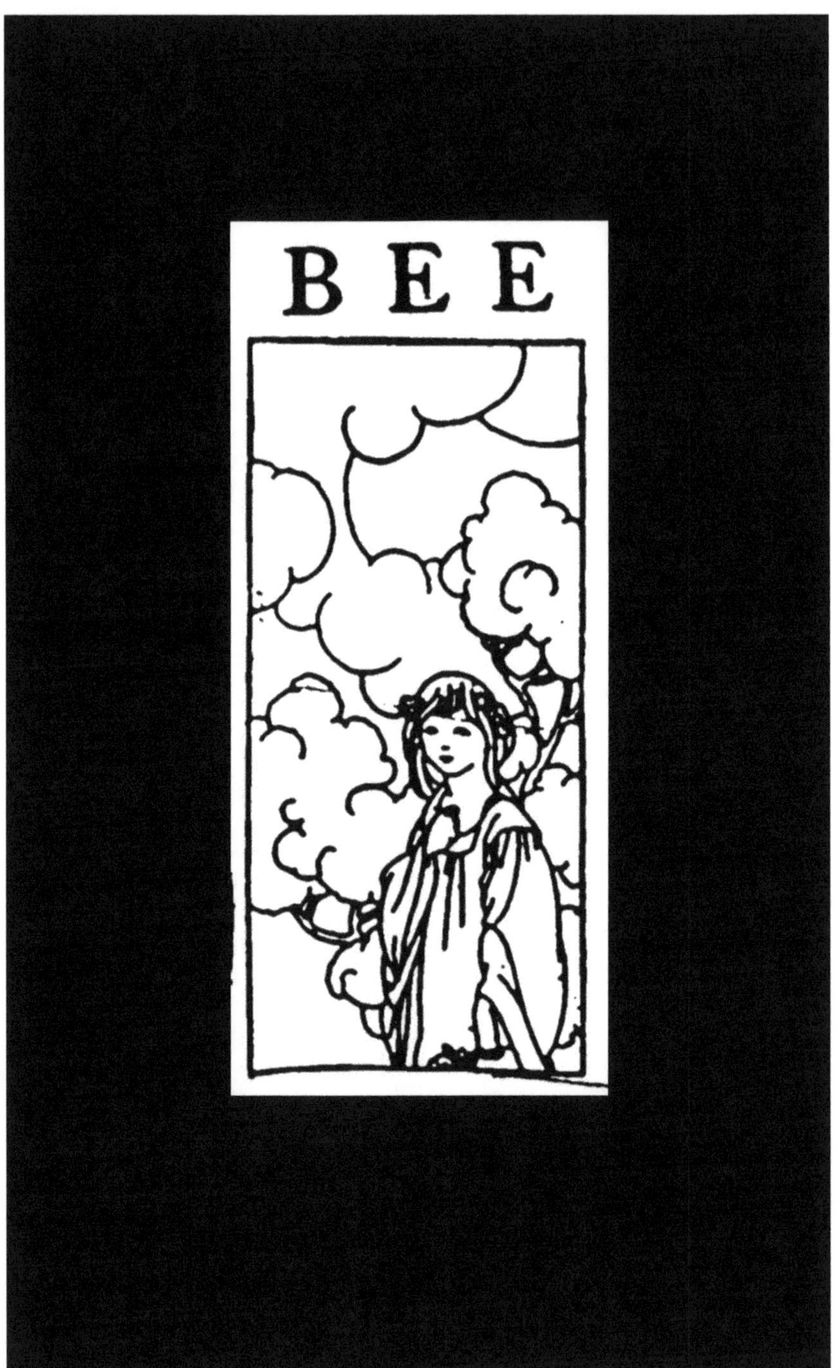
BEE

wild within wild

I don't belong
in the
crowded cafe
central station bustle
crammed city streets
shopping centres
peak hour tram rides home.

Give me
the desolate moors
of Exmoor
the cliffs
and rugged
Celtic Sea tide

I belong in the
oceans
of Byron
little Wategoes
where the dolphins swim

I don't belong
where only humans dwell.
Some part of me
smacks at the concrete artifice
we have made

Give me the lonely bush
of Eildon's high country
miles upon miles
of ghost gum
sanctuaries

the birds of my city home
they are my friends
they guide me, warn me,
laugh and giggle at me

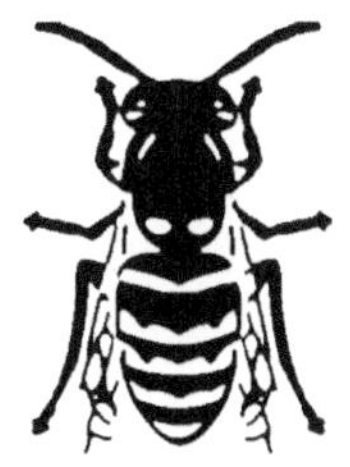

the neighbour's big husky
patrols our street
she has the eyes
of her ancestors

I am wary
alive
with her so near
(which is good)

broken-hearted misfit
belongs in the moors of home
where mum wrapped me
in scarves
in hats
in layers

cheeks whipped with wind
pink & fresh
eyes clear

I was
wild within wild.

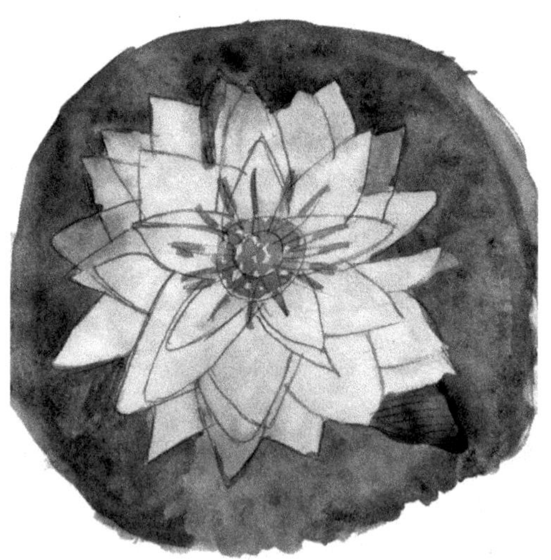

White Lotus by Bee

For Valley

Who you really are
is the child that does back-bends and cart-wheels
in the moist grass
while the dirt gets under your nails
and you bite it out slowly.

Who you really are
is the girl who ran her hands over her
new forming breasts
just to feel the softness of the skin.

Who you're really like
are those clowns that bend down
on one knee
and give you a flower
while they whack your bum when you're not looking
and trip you over.

Who you are really
becoming....is
unknown.

Yet when I feel you
you're like summer's hot nights,
like the breeze caressing.

You taste of salt
and the smell of the hot day sun
is in your hair.

You have rings on your toes.

And yet when it isn't this way,
when you're sad
when you're melancholy
this
you
rests.

BEE

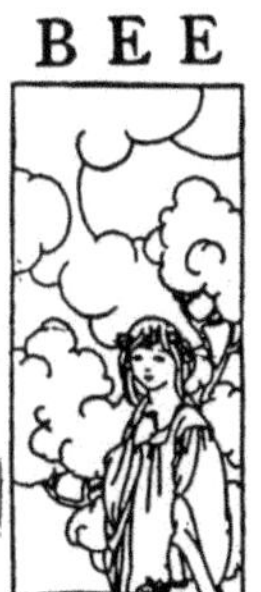

This you
curls up and waits
for the adult to drink down the world,
the world's changes
before it peels back the layers of doing
and the husk of generations
and leaps forth.

Like the dragonfly
tattooed on your shoulder
this
may
be
who you really are.

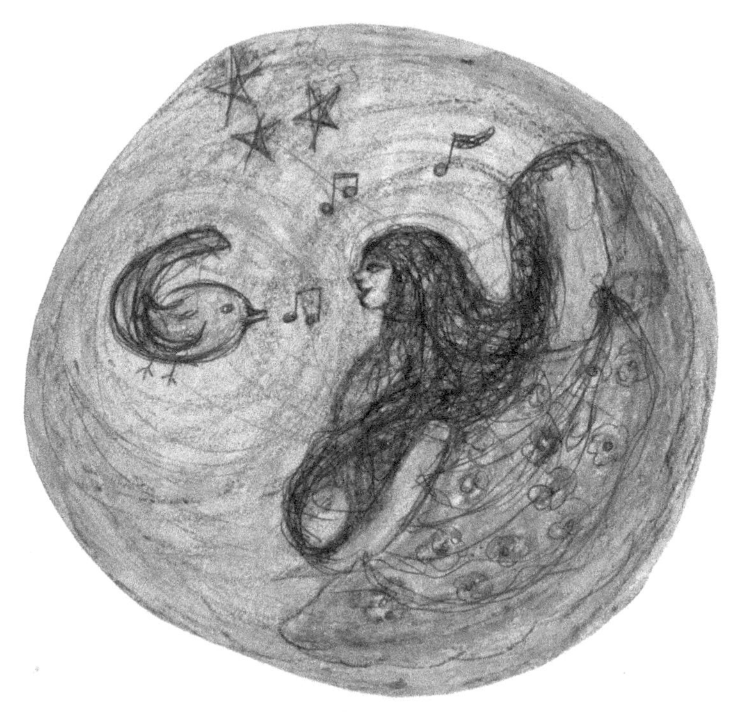

Bird Song by Naomi

My Soul Inhabits the Earth

Covered in briars and lichen
buried for thousands of years
my soul comes
uncovered.

From the depths of my dreaming
buried for an eternity
it comes
surfing
on the night's
coral sea
swinging
through
the earth's
soaring nebulae.

Covered in moss and mud
dreaming of things
concealed.

My soul
She comes to me.

Sinking beneath the waves
of despair
of emptiness
where this is
both
emptiness
and
the
other.

I lie
foetal and coiled,
extracted coldly
of all hopes.

vibed by the city's
angst.

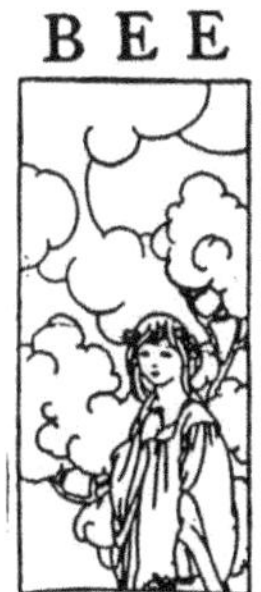

There is no peace here.

Wrapped in blankets of cold,
earthly deception.

No mystery.

Shivering from the womb
out
in it
already.

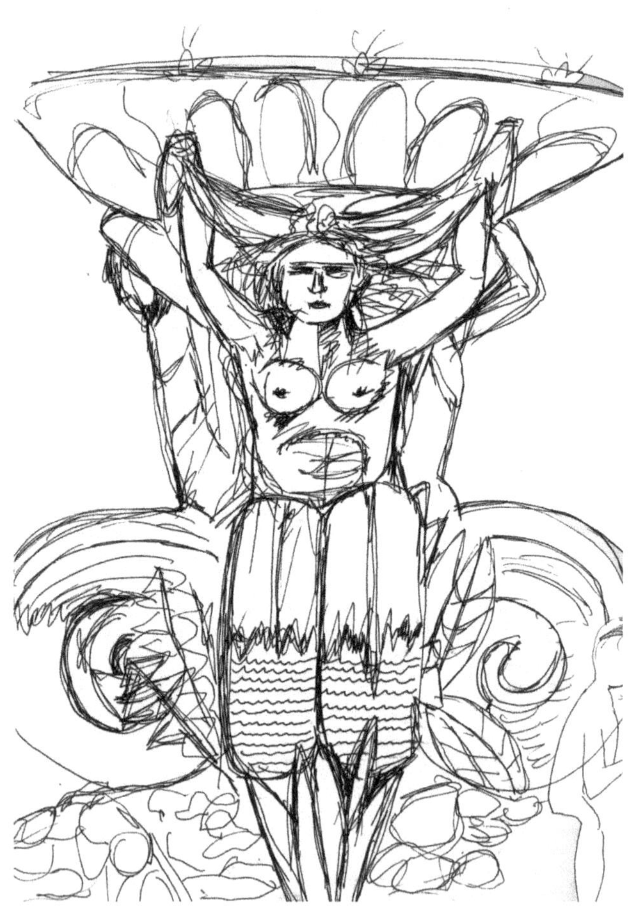

City Fountain Sketch by Bee

Terra Nullius

Tens of Thousands of Years

one country
one land
one people

One Hundred Years

pioneers
loggers
buildings
cities
rent
petrol
gas
electricity
cars
goldmines

an island
a country
ruined

destroyed
raped and left
for dead

One Hundred Years

rampant consumerism
white is right
the mindless acquiring of wealth

Our First World Paradise

pesticides
insecticides
oil refineries
coal stations

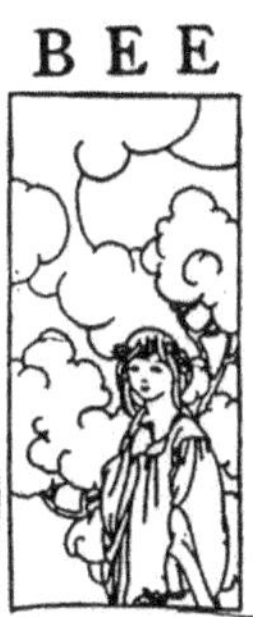

soil salinity
blue green algae
freeways
housing estates
asylums
institutions

hum hum hum

the bee's
turn blue and green,
grow seven wings
eleven eyes

mutant honey-makers

from fire makers, dream brothers,
family and a sacred land

loved with each hand
of each generation

Tens of Thousands of Years
here, right here

One Hundred Years
Only One Hundred Years

what have we left you?
WHAT HAVE WE LEFT YOU?

plastic bottles
plastic bags
choking the Merri
trickles
where once was rushing
the Snowy

Ancient moonlight, ghost gums
cleared with no thought
no thought
of tomorrows loves needs wants

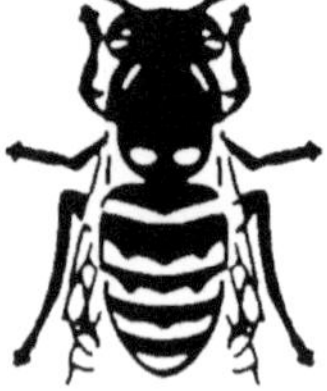

It's my passion

My body sprawls listlessly
in this big bed,
the passion
remains unspent.

I want
you to
take me

But you're lounging
On the other side,
A "friend", that's all
you say.

You're Icarus, descended.
A quiet myth, lounging.

But
I want
more.

I want
to feel you
from inside.

You're a stranger still,
to these honey drenched thighs.

It is me
Imaging a body
Convulsing with pleasure.

Skin to teeth to hair,
To places I never dared.

I want
To ripple with pleasure,
The nauseating, agonising,
Tingling warmth
Never leaves me.

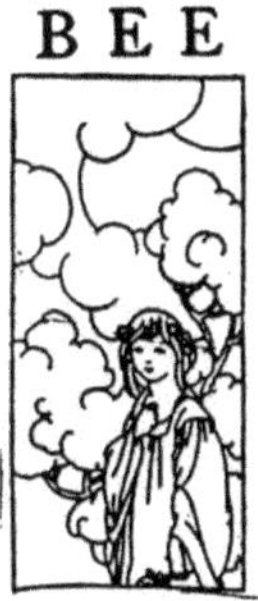

Wrap those writhing arms
Around this waist,
Pulling me up
Till I ascend you,
And you are driven
Deeper in me.

Feel the
stiff
thumb
press

Smoothly the spine.

Savour
the
double-tonguing
Of thigh on thigh

Wet on eye
ear
and
mouth.

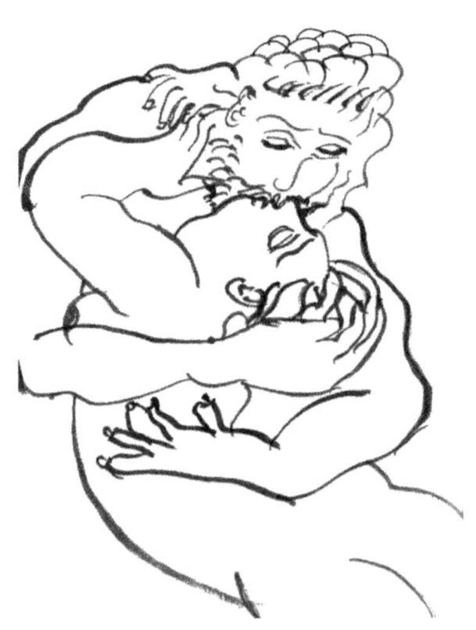

Lovers (inspired by Picasso) by Bee

On and Off

It's raining
last night the cafe was dark
you were standing, I was tired.
What is this fear
it keeps me here writing.

Your strange face suddenly appears
in the mask of your unshed tears.

We cannot speak
but those eyes
they cry sorrow.

I am afraid
the thing that keeps me close also drives me away.
The paradox of attraction.

I lose myself in days of fruitless
yet euphoric fantasies.
Erotic and placid, together,
on the bench in my mind,
called love.

It grows larger every day
expectation.
Chips flake away from the varnished surface.
I try to spit shine the layers of illusion
simultaneously on and off.

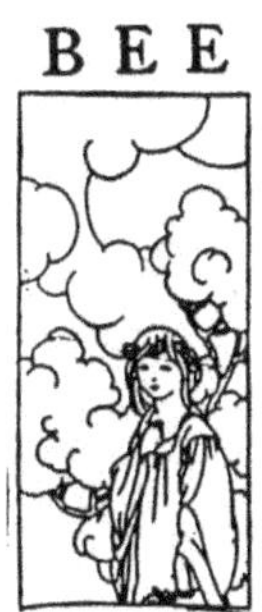

A Note to God

My truth
turns
gold
in your Garden
Your precious soul is here
as I look
as I know
it is time
I am opening your book
it is my life
a sacred turning towards
your Love
Your gifts of fruit and flowers
words and music
are Love

A River Somewhere

To be still
naked
floating
in a river
somewhere.

Tea Poem

the satori of tea

the samadhi of water

the ecstasy of liquid

the divine union of minerals

the moksha of molecules

the balance of energy

the end result?

the bliss of small things

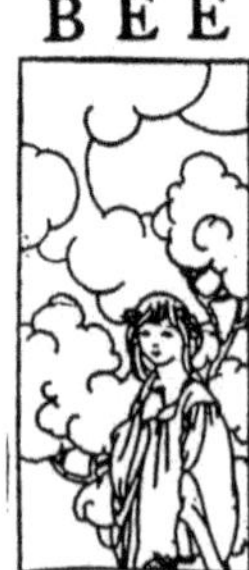

My Lover

Yesterday.
Yesterday I suppressed my pain,
and the frustration
turned to
anger.

Today?
Today my sorrow
is deeper than to
cry,
but
I do not
question why,
but rather,
when?
When did your memories
die?
Or did they
just
fade?

Tomorrow?
Tomorrow I lie alone,
but in
my arms
you will
be
sleeping.

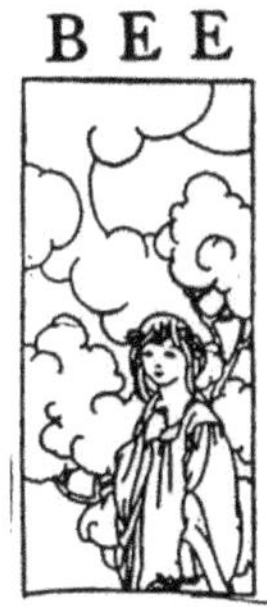

(written when 14 years old)

Standing back from the Mountain

The day before last
I was at the edge
I was on the cliff
staring down the waves
and the winds

I did not seek this out
I did not go looking
for madness

I use everything I can muster
to step back off the mountain,
inch my way back
step by small step

I visualise etheric colours,
white with a band of gold
as I have been told
this protects

I even use 'facebook'
to focus for moments
and a man's story screams out to be heard

I listen at 11pm
in a mauve flannelette bed
to his story of pancreatic cancer
only a month or two left
3 young kids left behind

I try to hold the rope
leading home
to sanity and faith

I read the wave poem
my epic book
no-one has seen

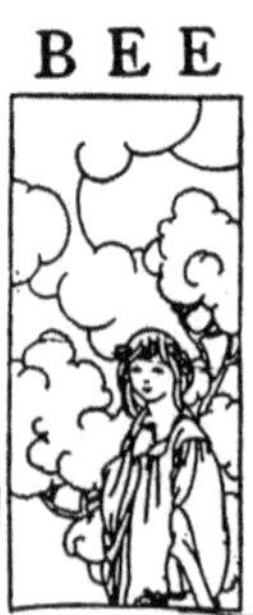

I use lullabies
hot waterbottles
rose water
and stuart wilde

and I find myself
now
breathing
slower
and
feeling
my feet

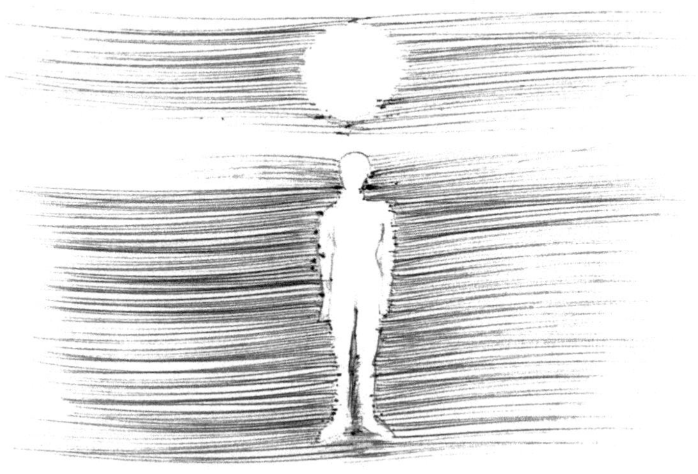

therapise me again doctor by Bee

Crone

A strong old woman awoke
The crone she spoke
ahhh, she told me to leave my bed
Out to the garden I was led
To meet the thunder
And talk of the Poetry of Sin

An ugly old crone spoke
she cackled away
She was twisted
And new
Both brittle and warm

Tears of joy
joining bonds
I wept at meeting her
At last
A woman
A mother

the Crone
A woman of disgrace
Gaudy and black
I have faith in the "Grand-mother"

I am in true regret
of never having known you
till now

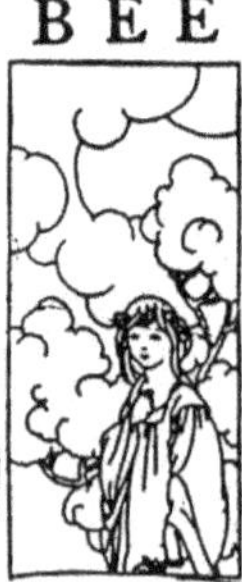

I know Om

She's a little girl
On a precipice
A great divining thought

I saw Om on the ocean
Sheath

everything's perfect
a beautiful paradox
existed
I am One with all
That she has created
All that I touch with
my hands are beauteous
for she made it so
even this
this book
is a gift from heaven

where the fuck is heaven?
who knows

I'm in heaven
Right now
Write now
Right now

My tiny garden
It speaks
To me
Very stript back
Beaten
Bleeding
Knowing
Come

She moves all things

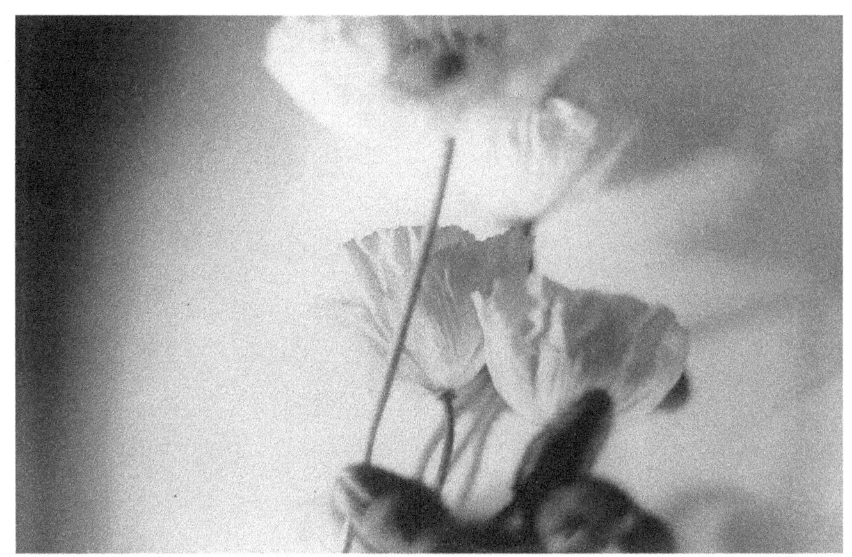

Poppies for Henry I by Bee

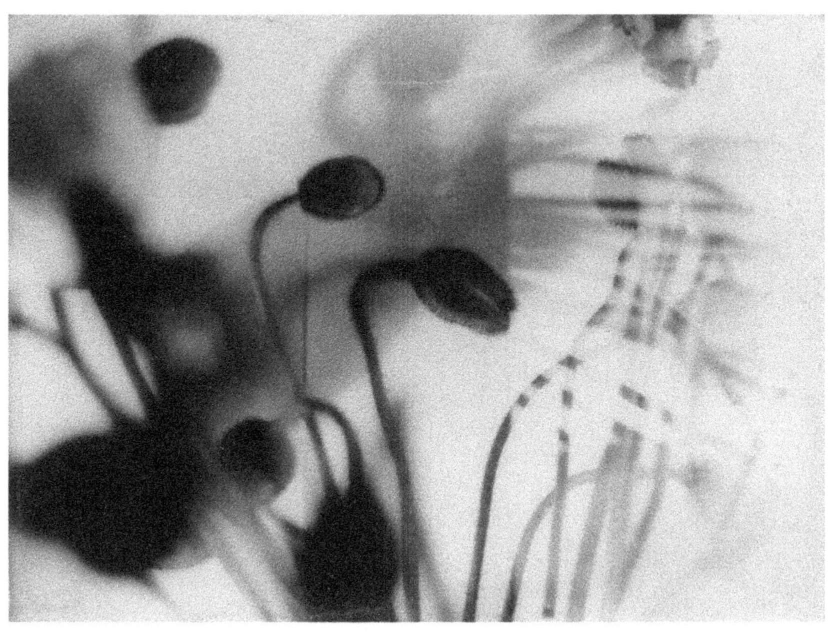

Poppies for Henry II by Bee

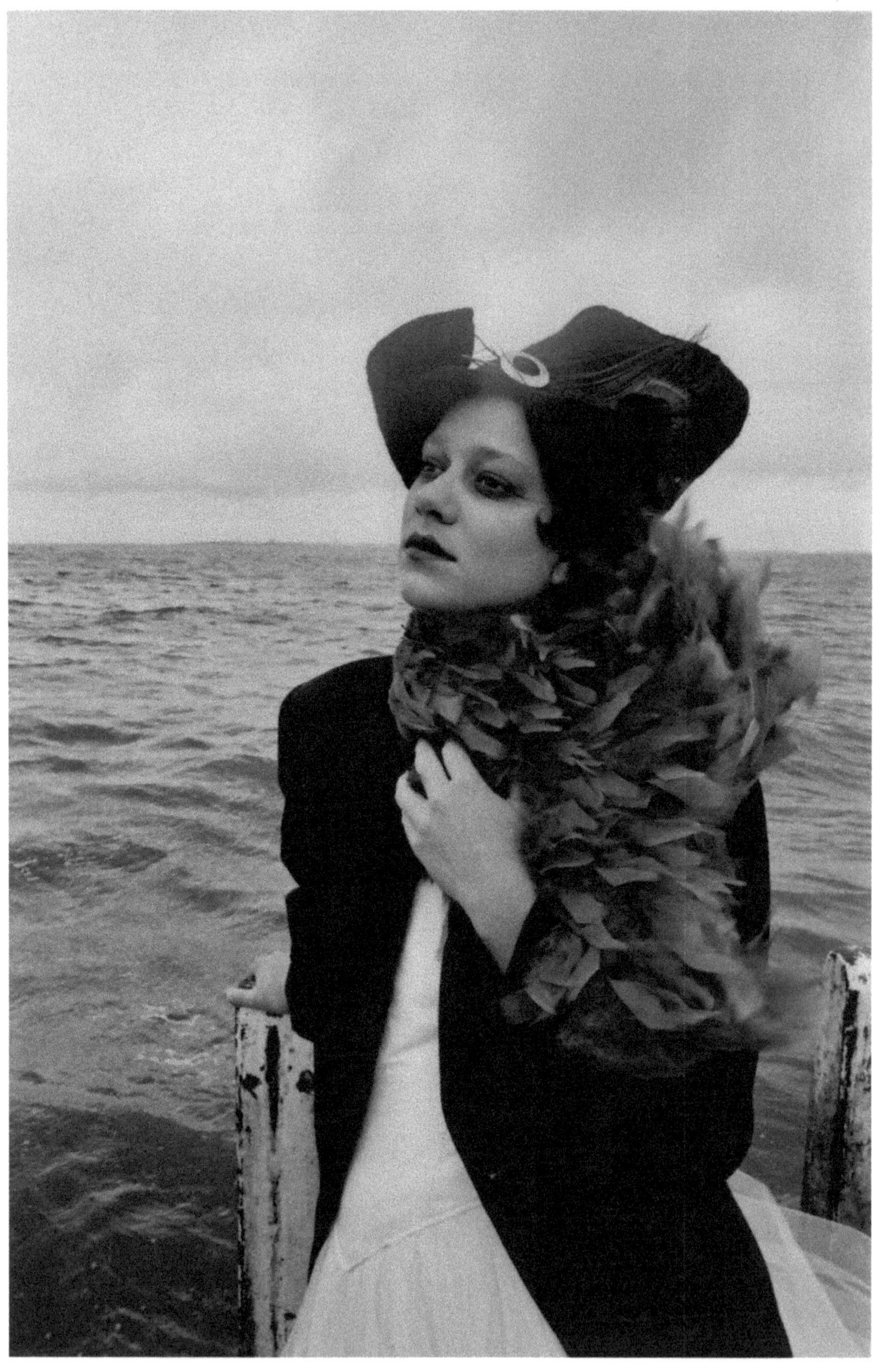

Sophia by Bee

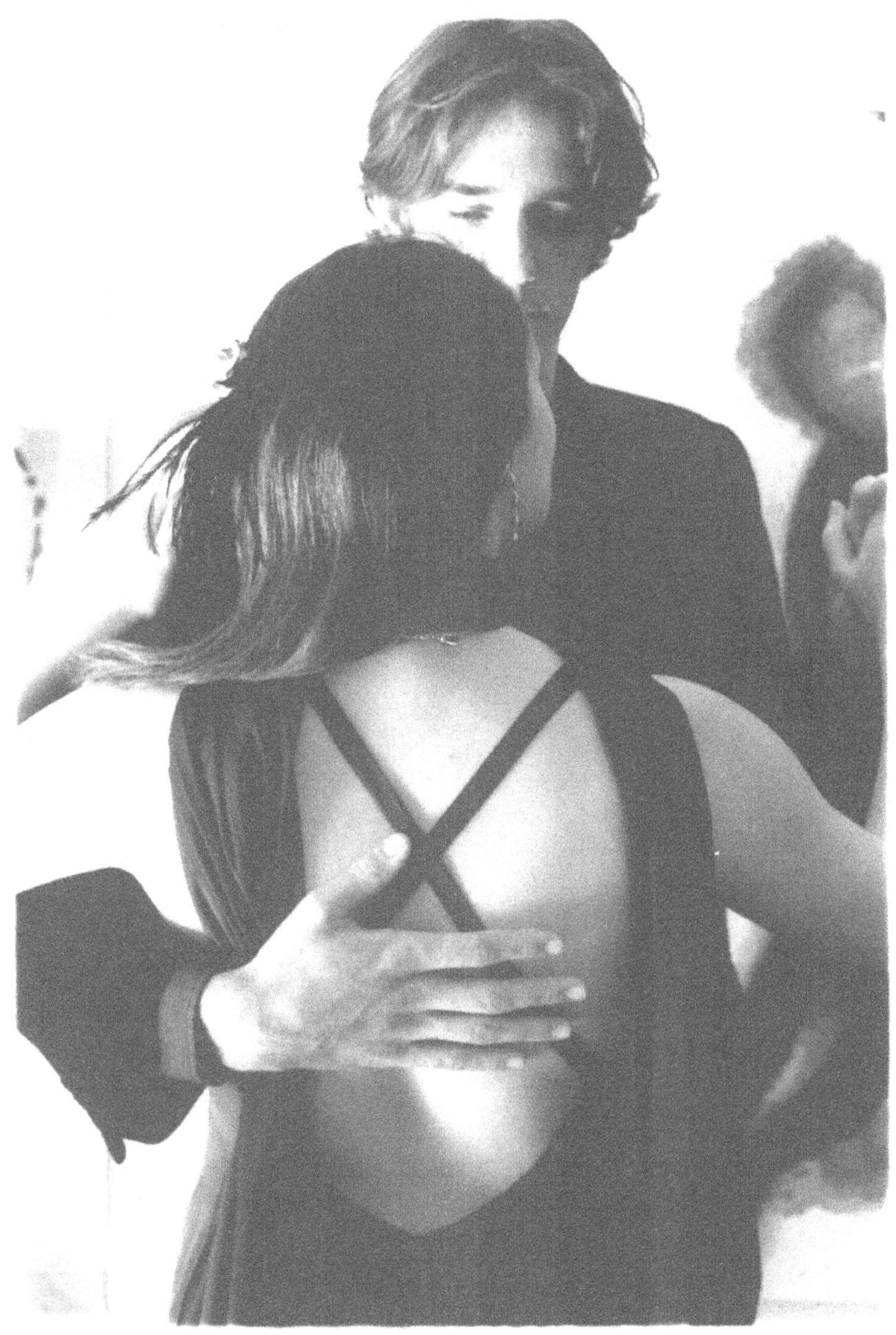

Love Dancers by Bee

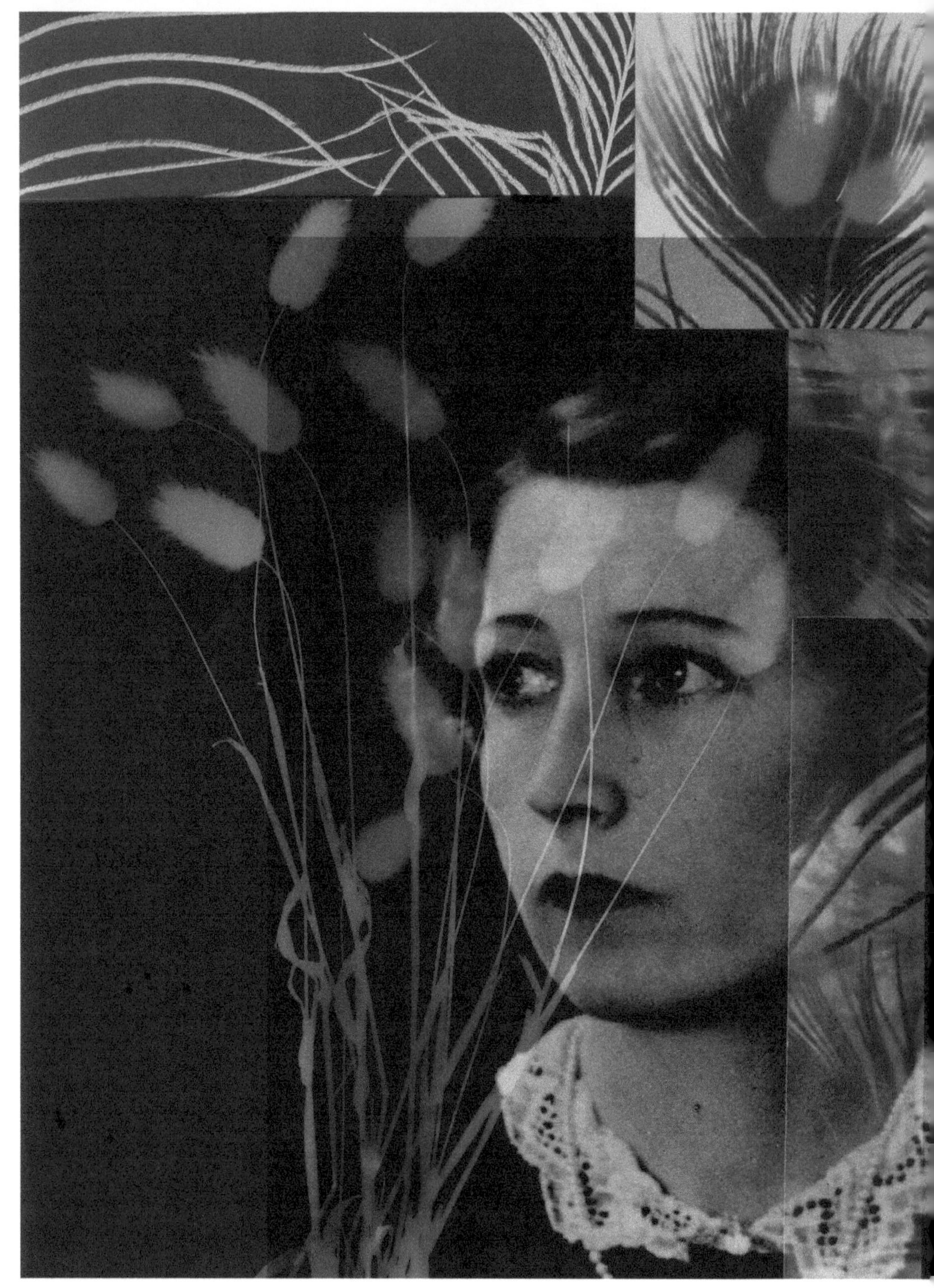

30 Grandmother Winifred by Bee

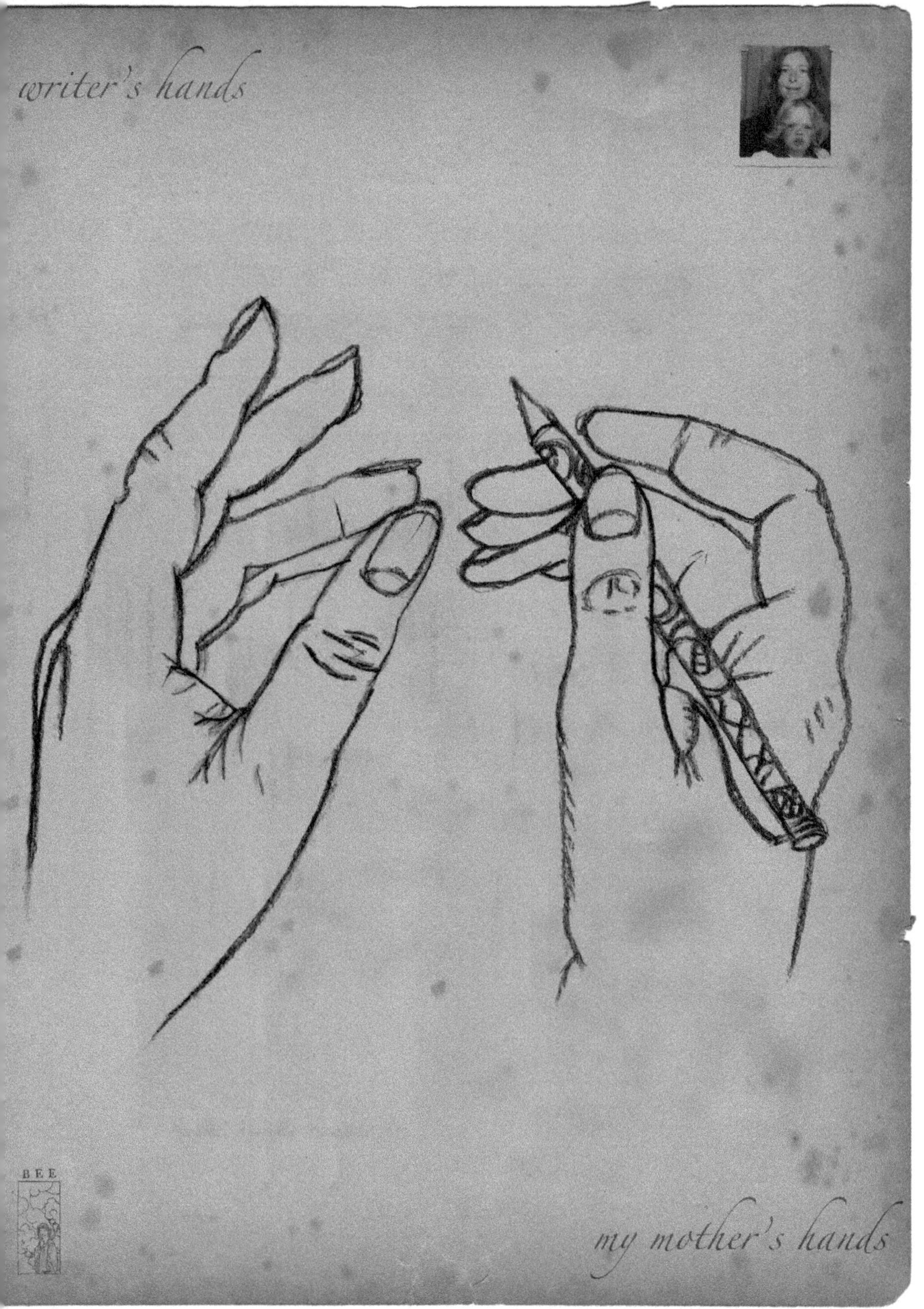
writer's hands
BEE
my mother's hands

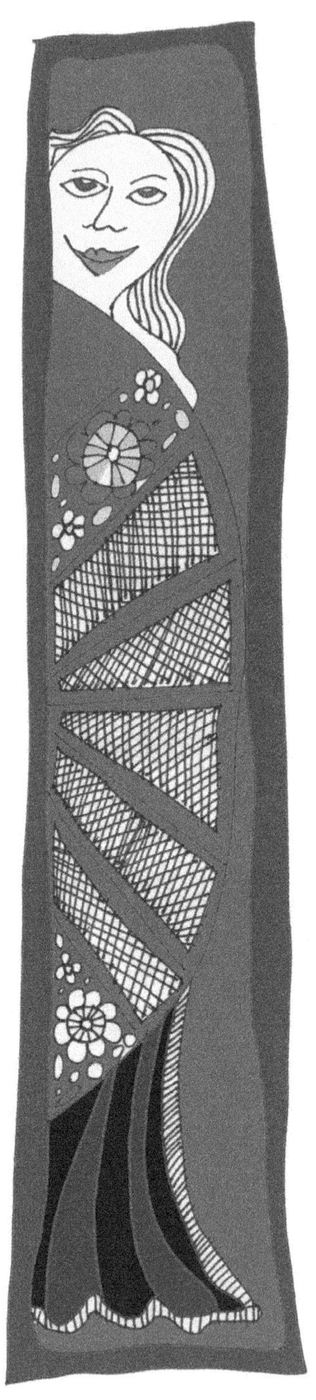
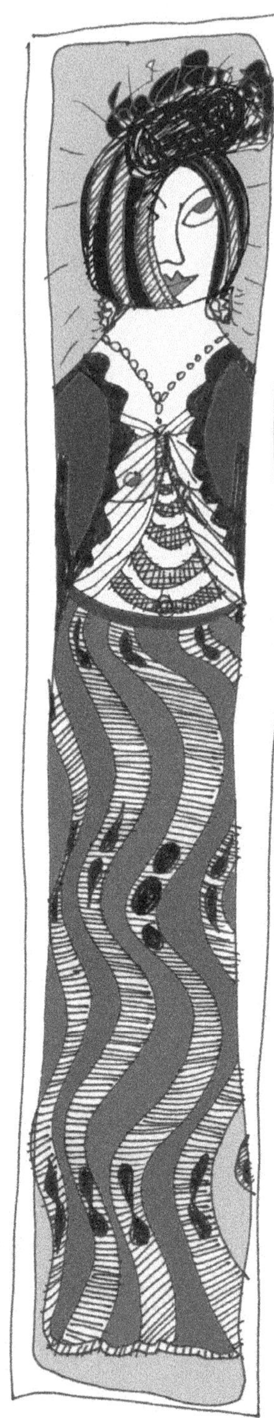
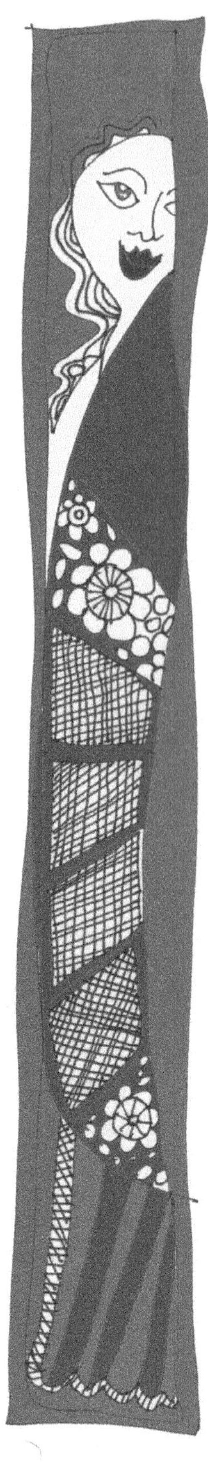

 Three Art Deco Ladies by Bee

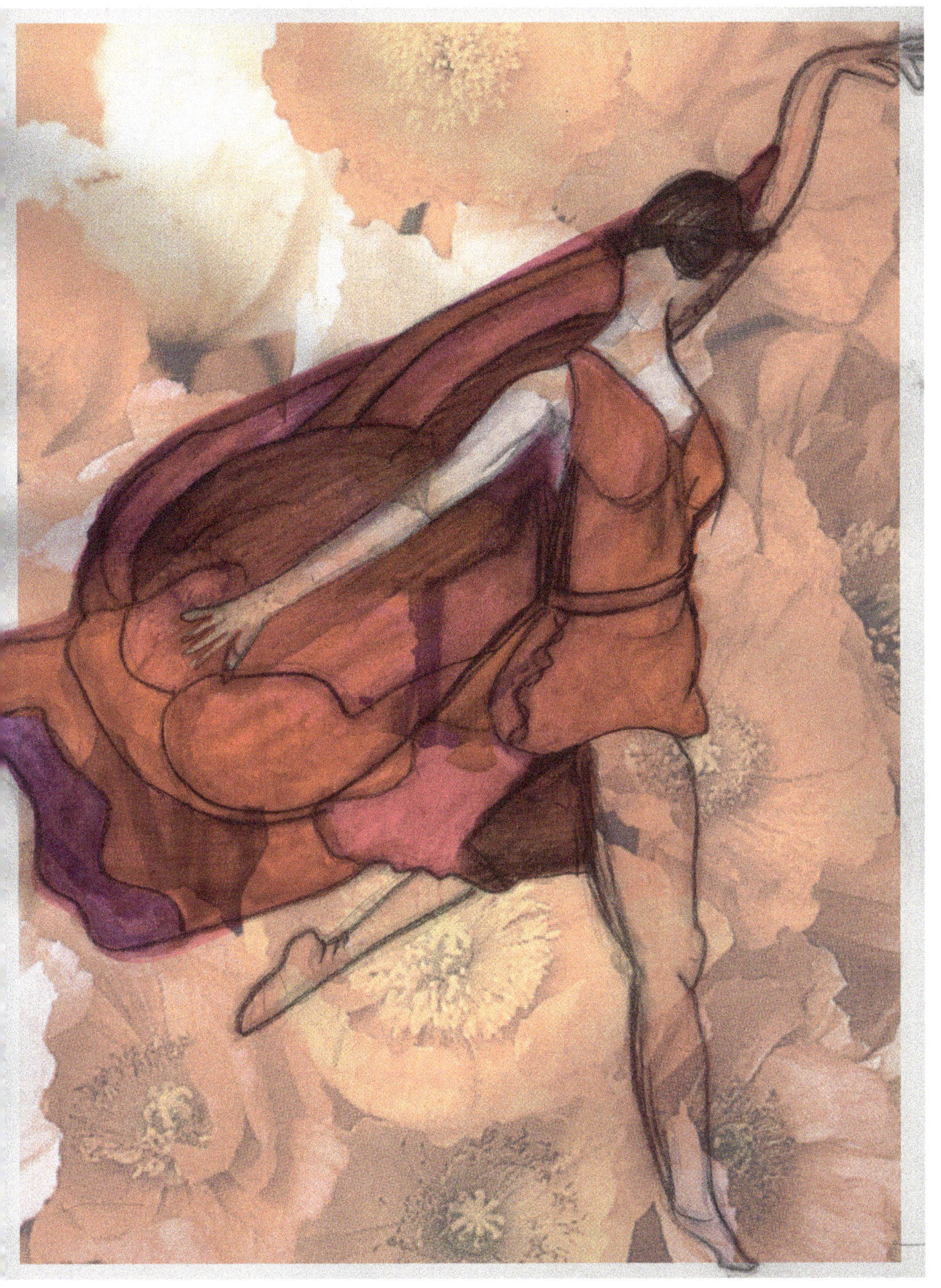

For Auntie Anne Duncan by Bee

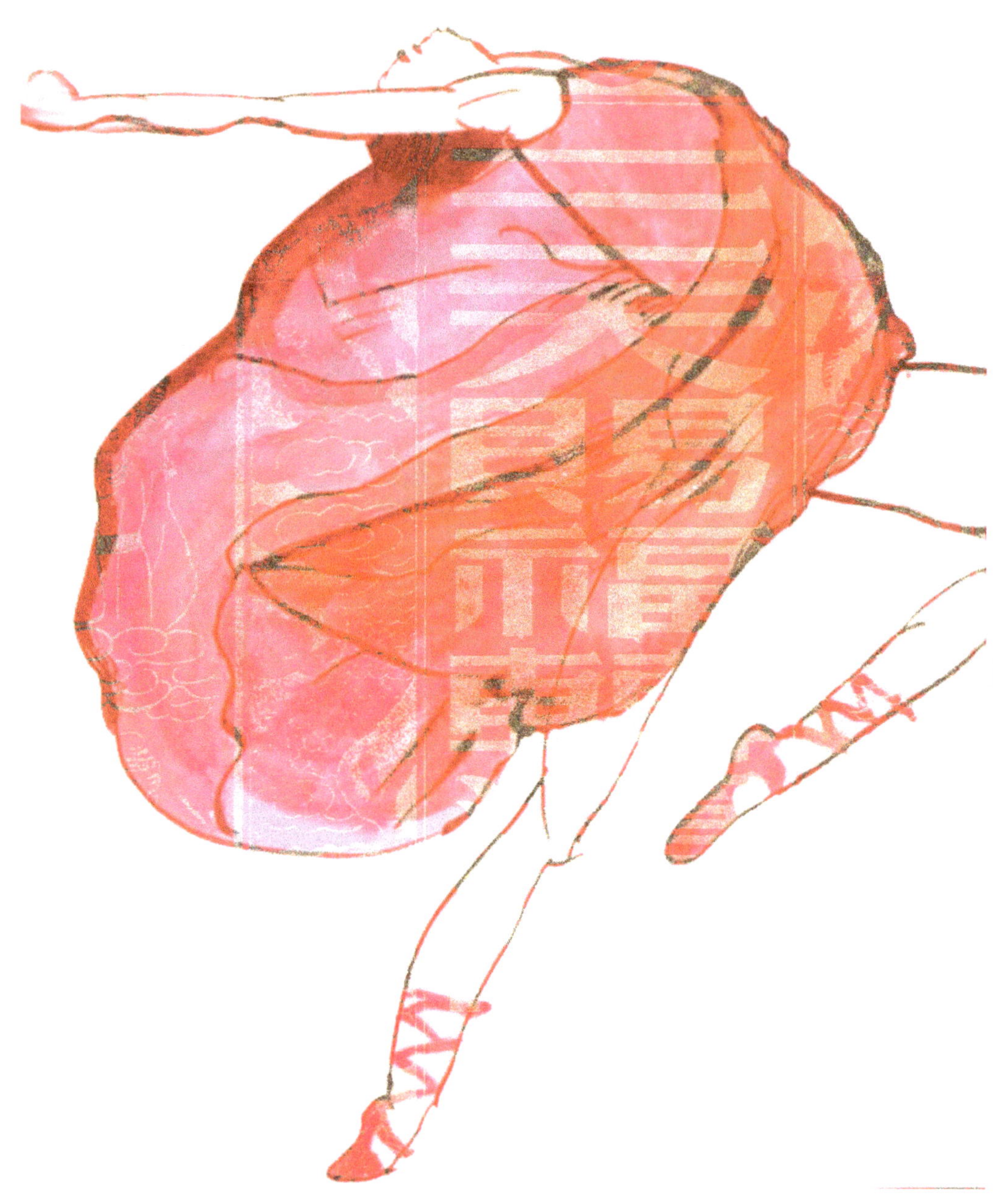

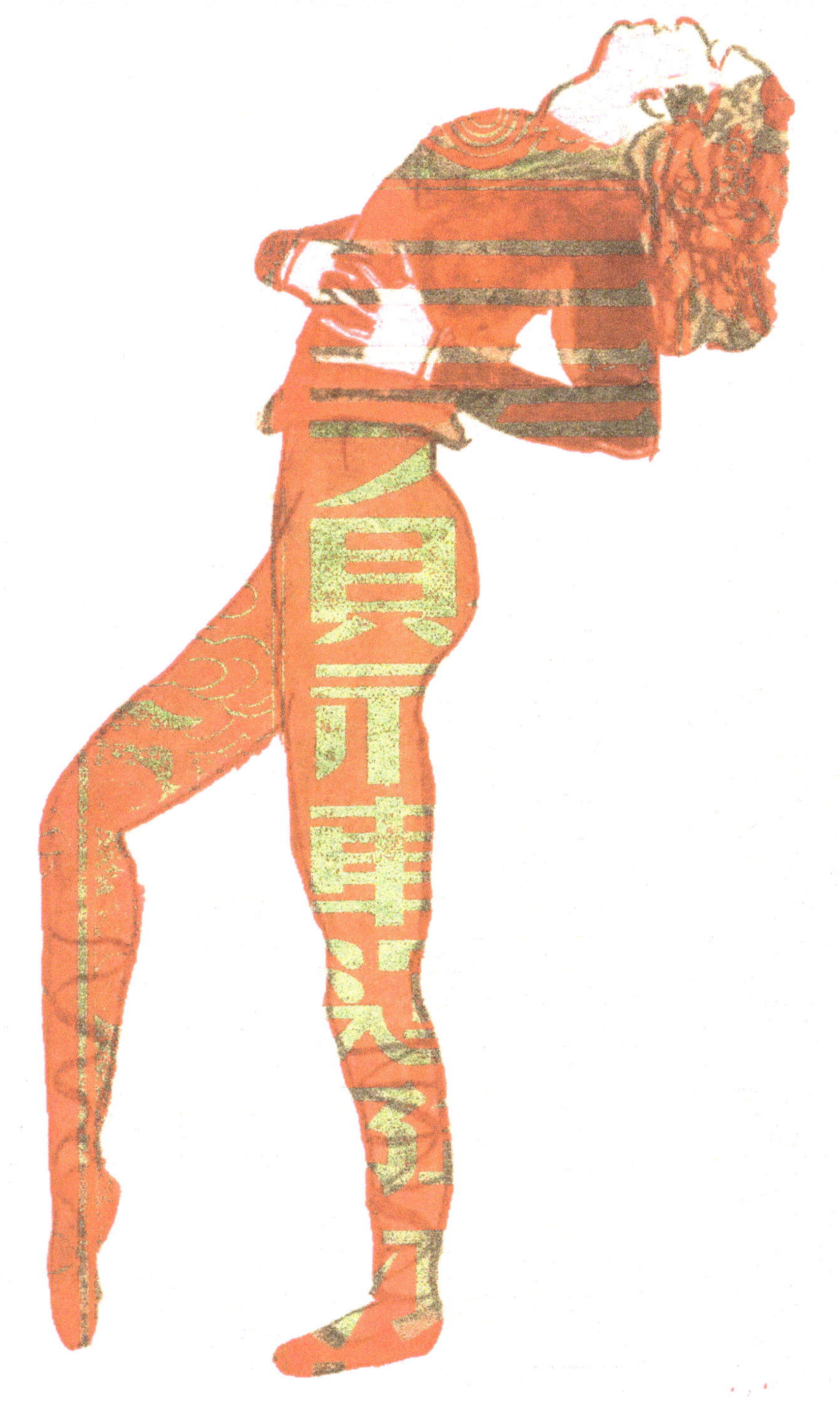

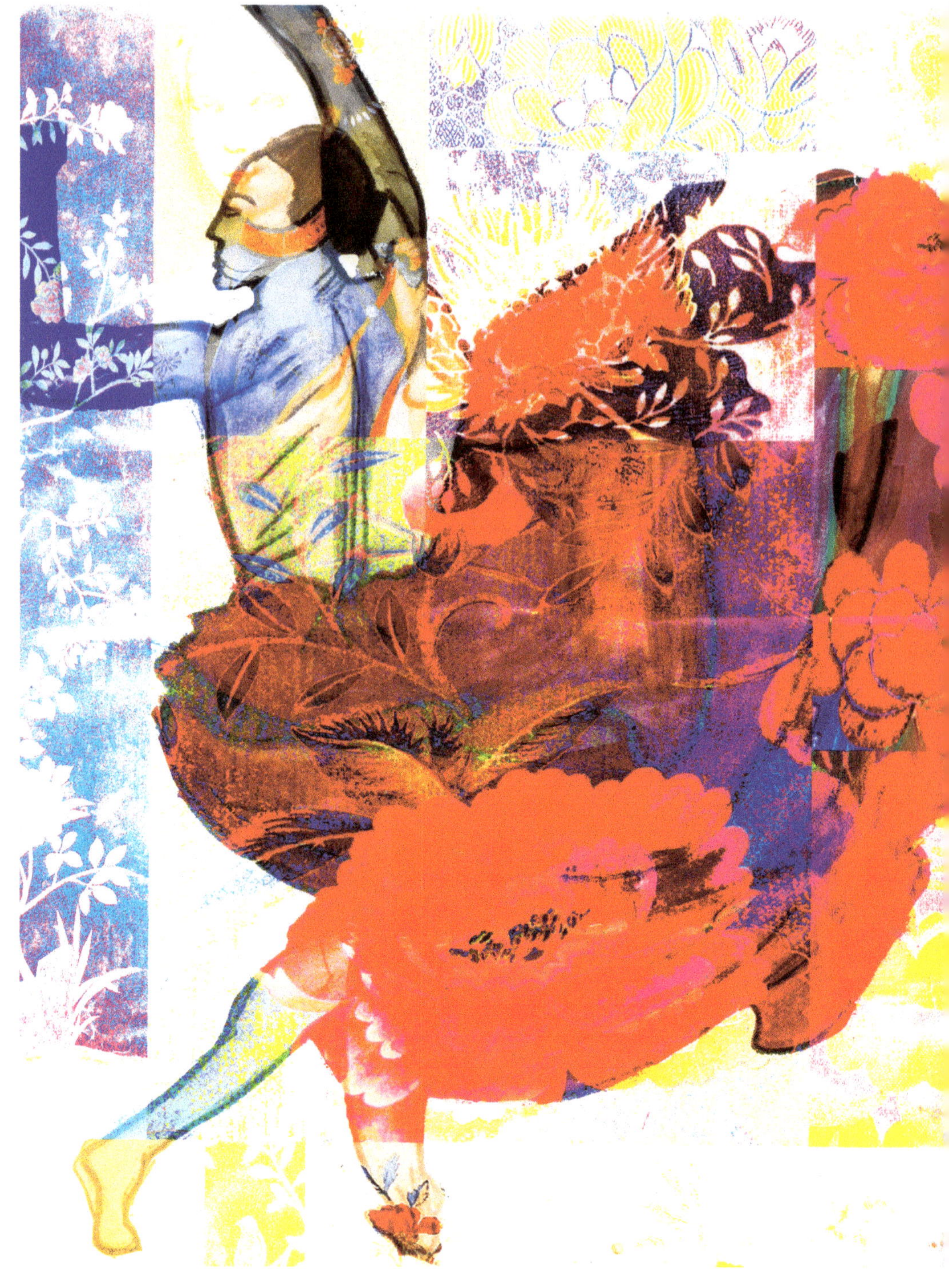

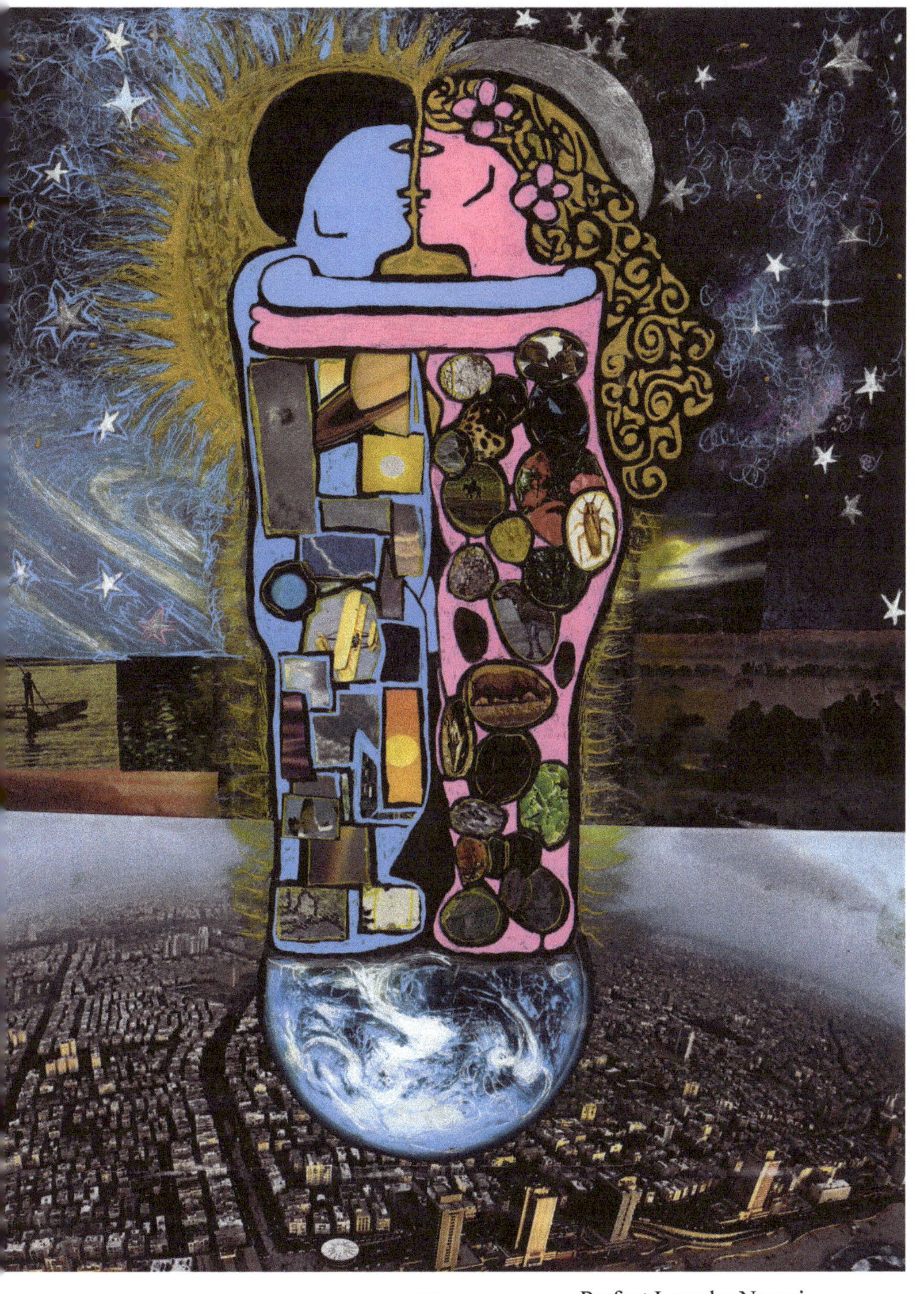

Perfect Love by Naomi

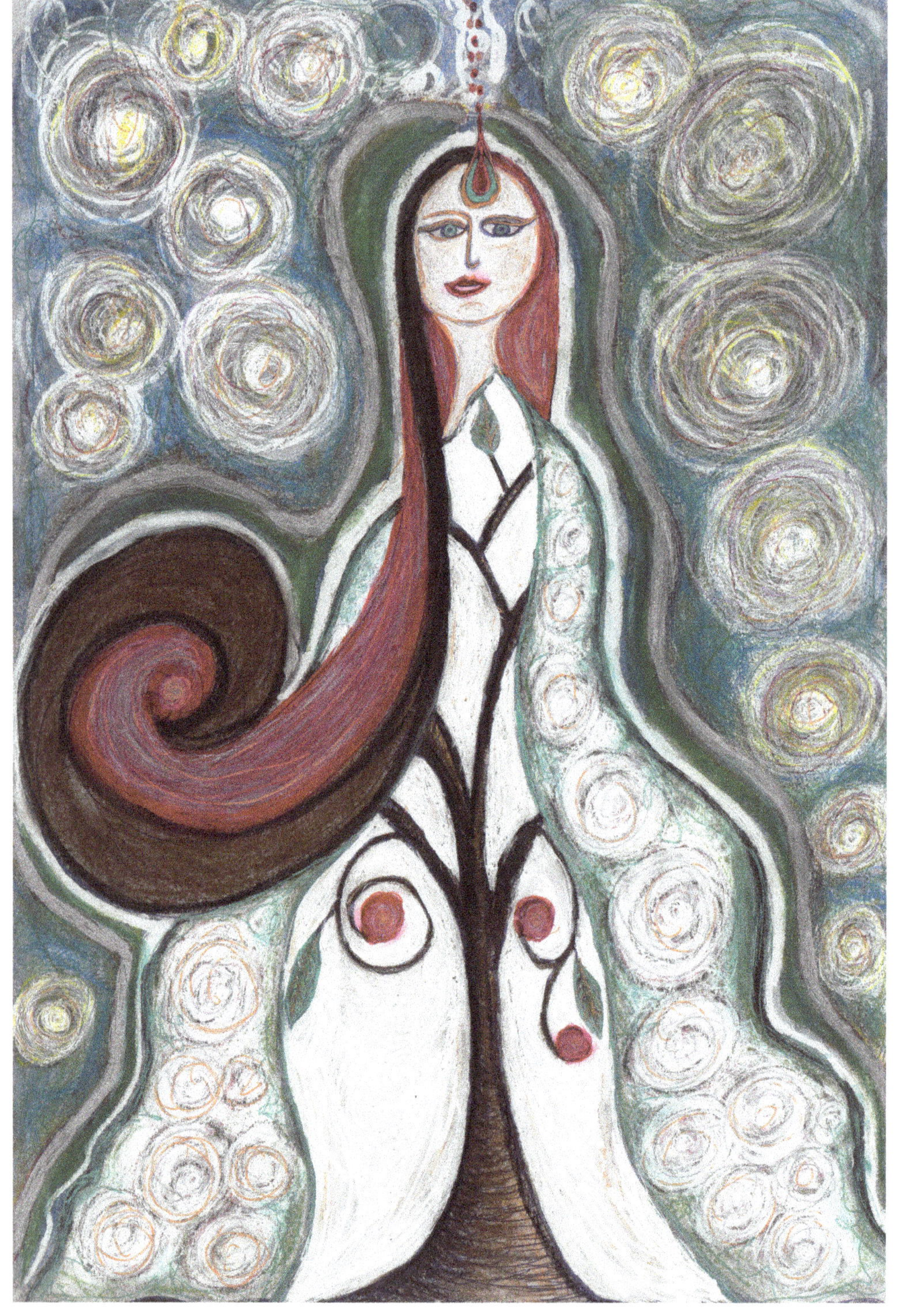

 Lady of Wisdom by Naomi

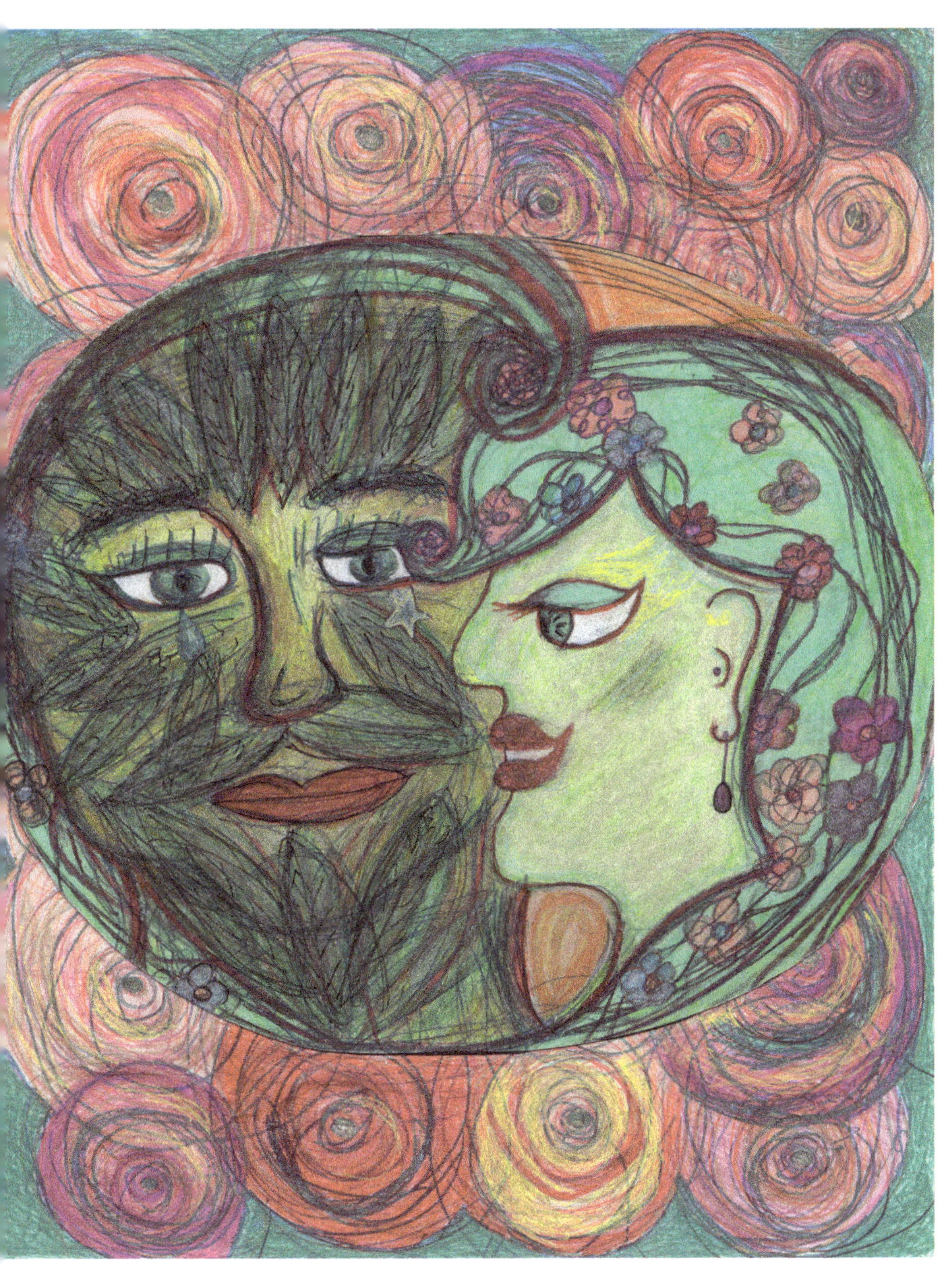

 Green Man and Lady of Blossoms by Naomi

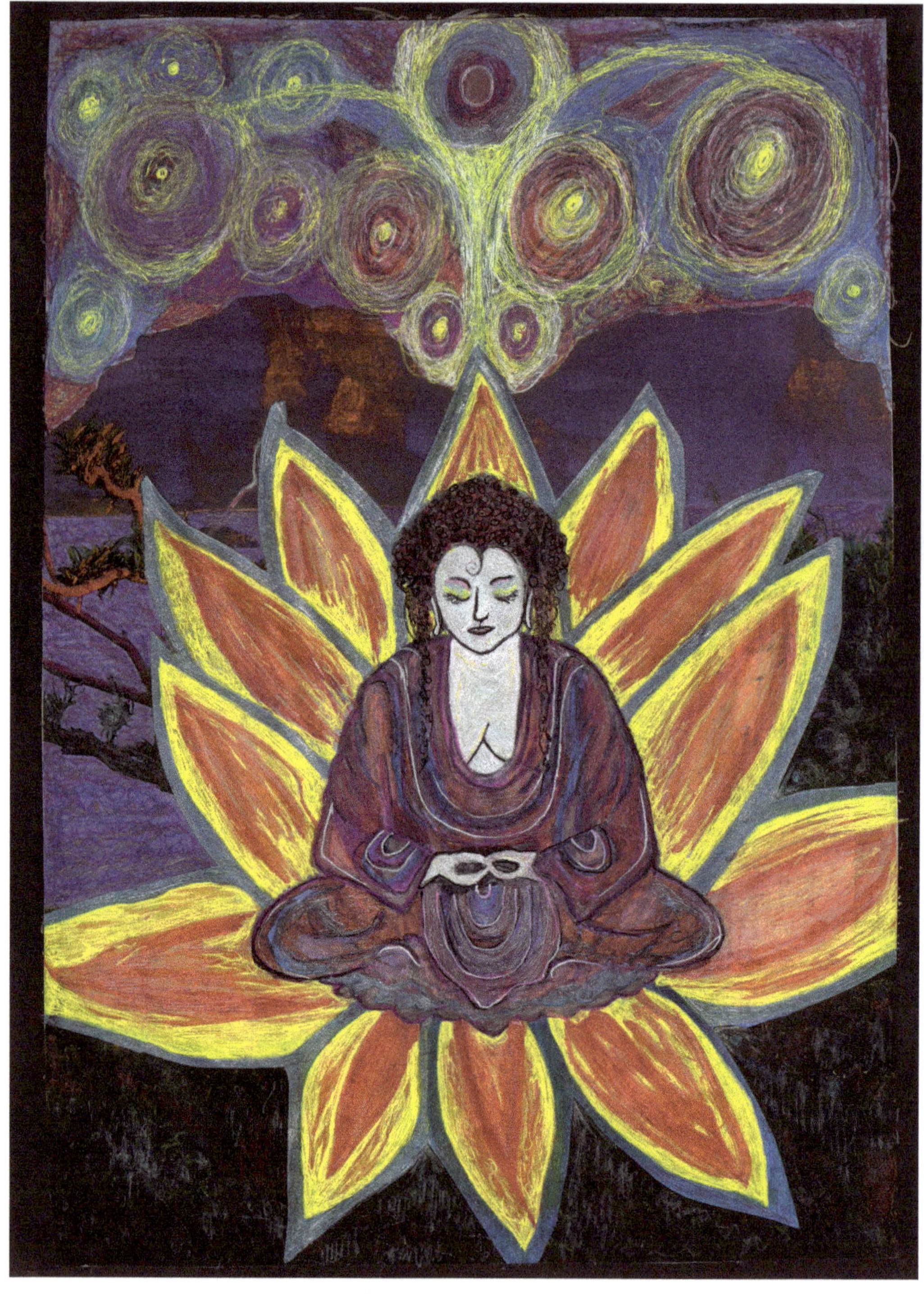

 Shining Light by Naomi

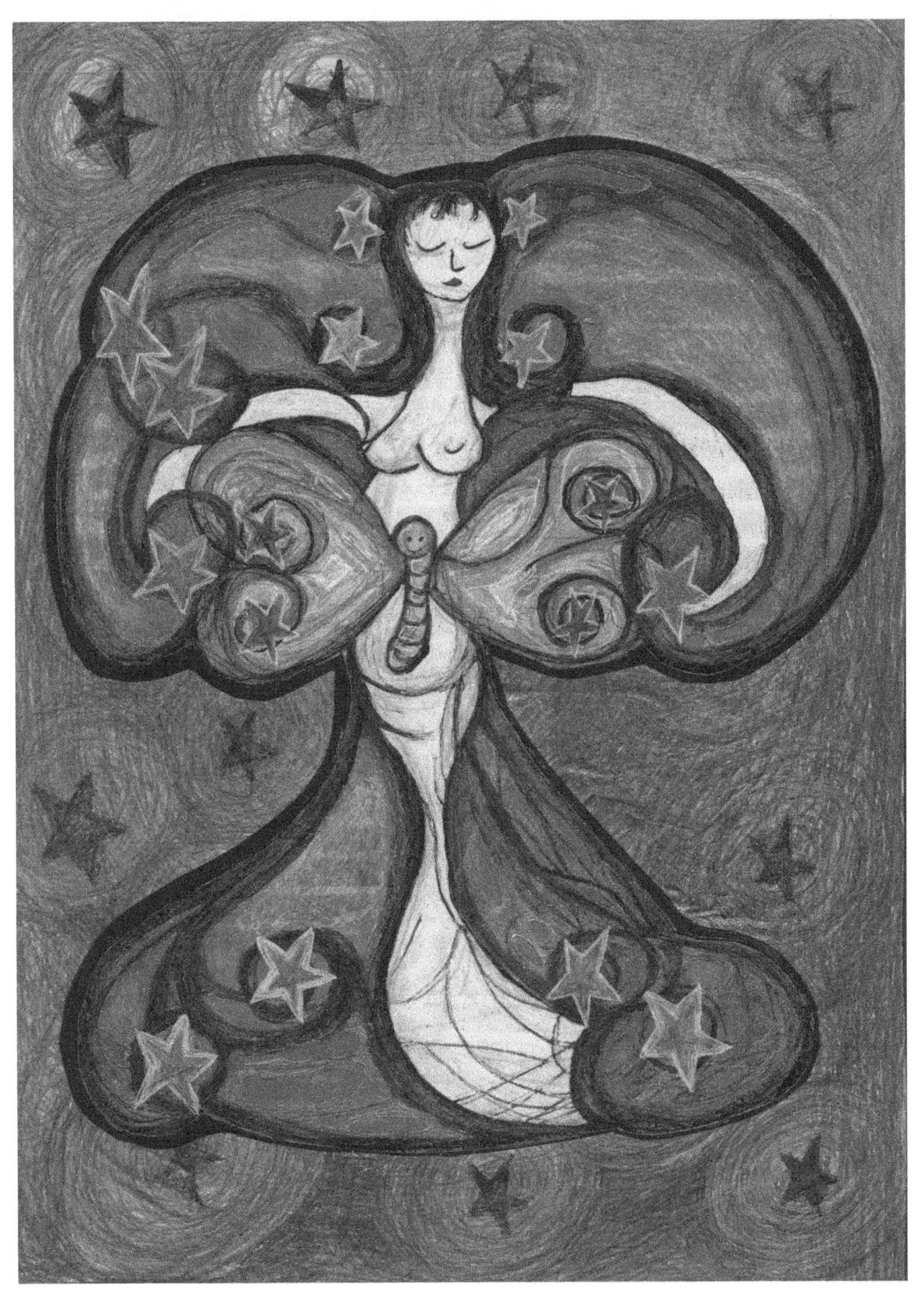

 Tree Woman Dreaming by Naomi

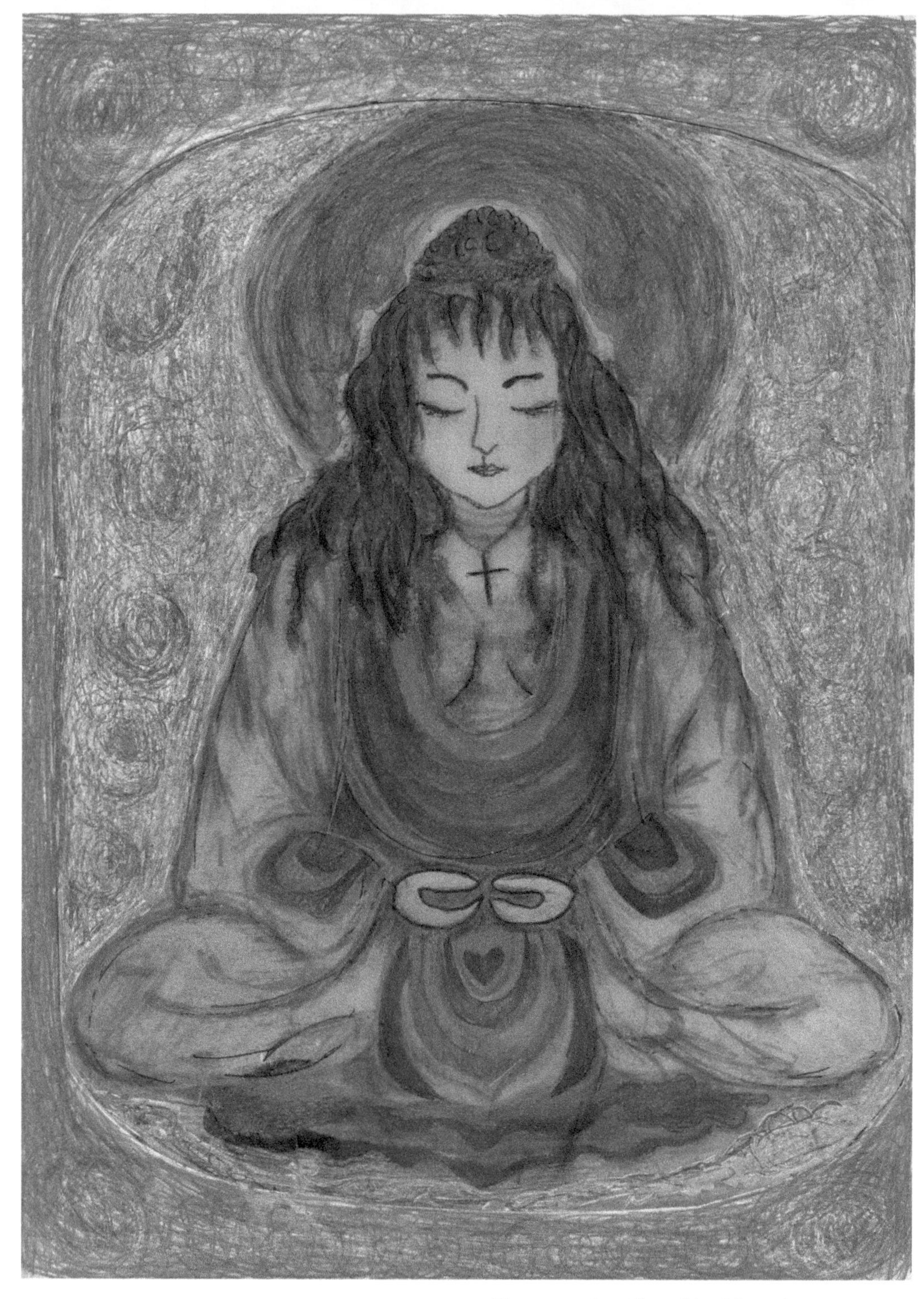

 Om Shanti by Naomi

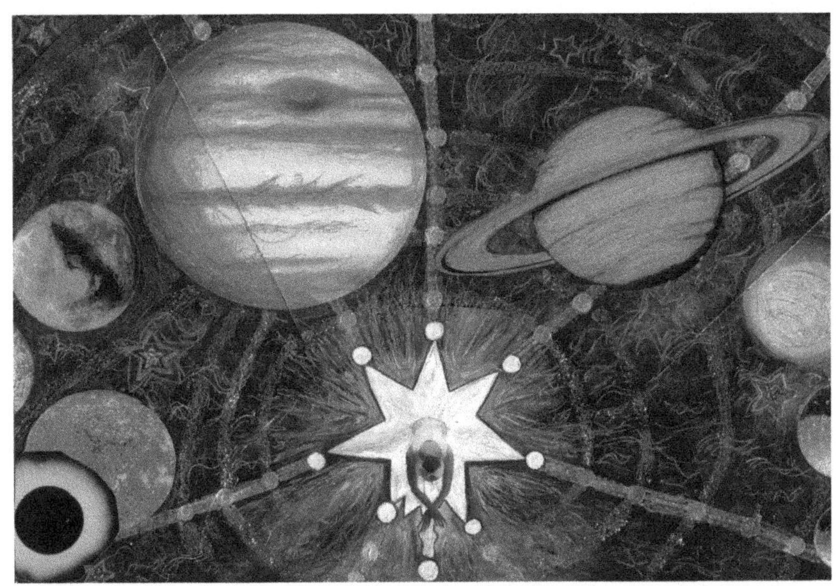

Web of Life by Naomi

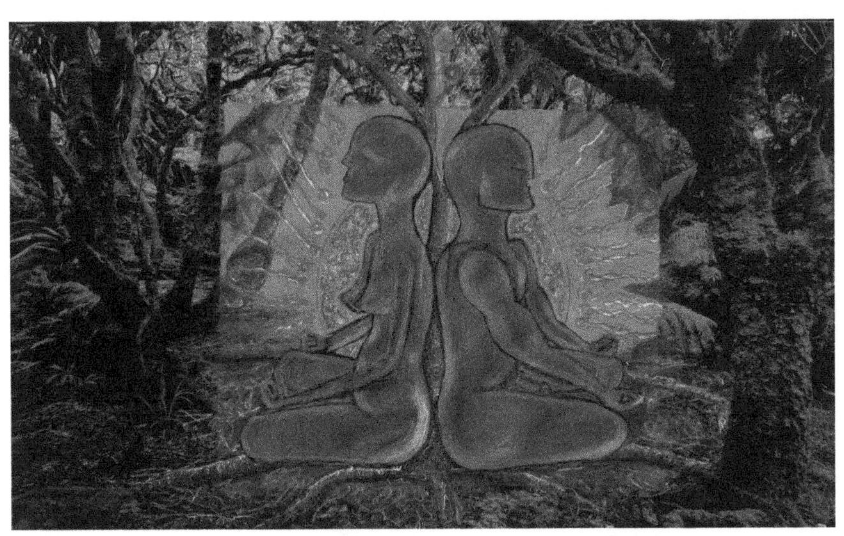

Adam & Eve by Naomi

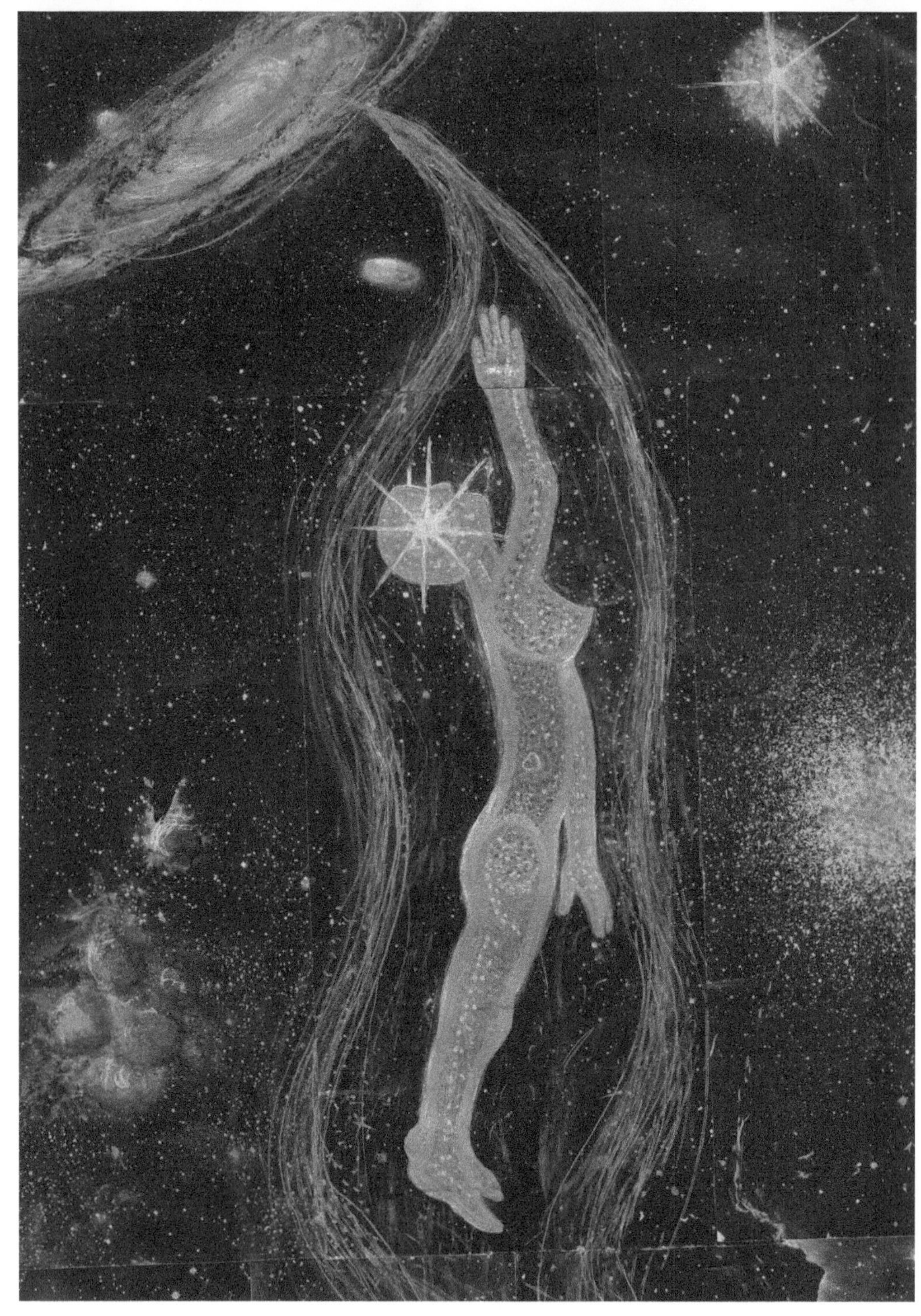

Star Travel by Naomi

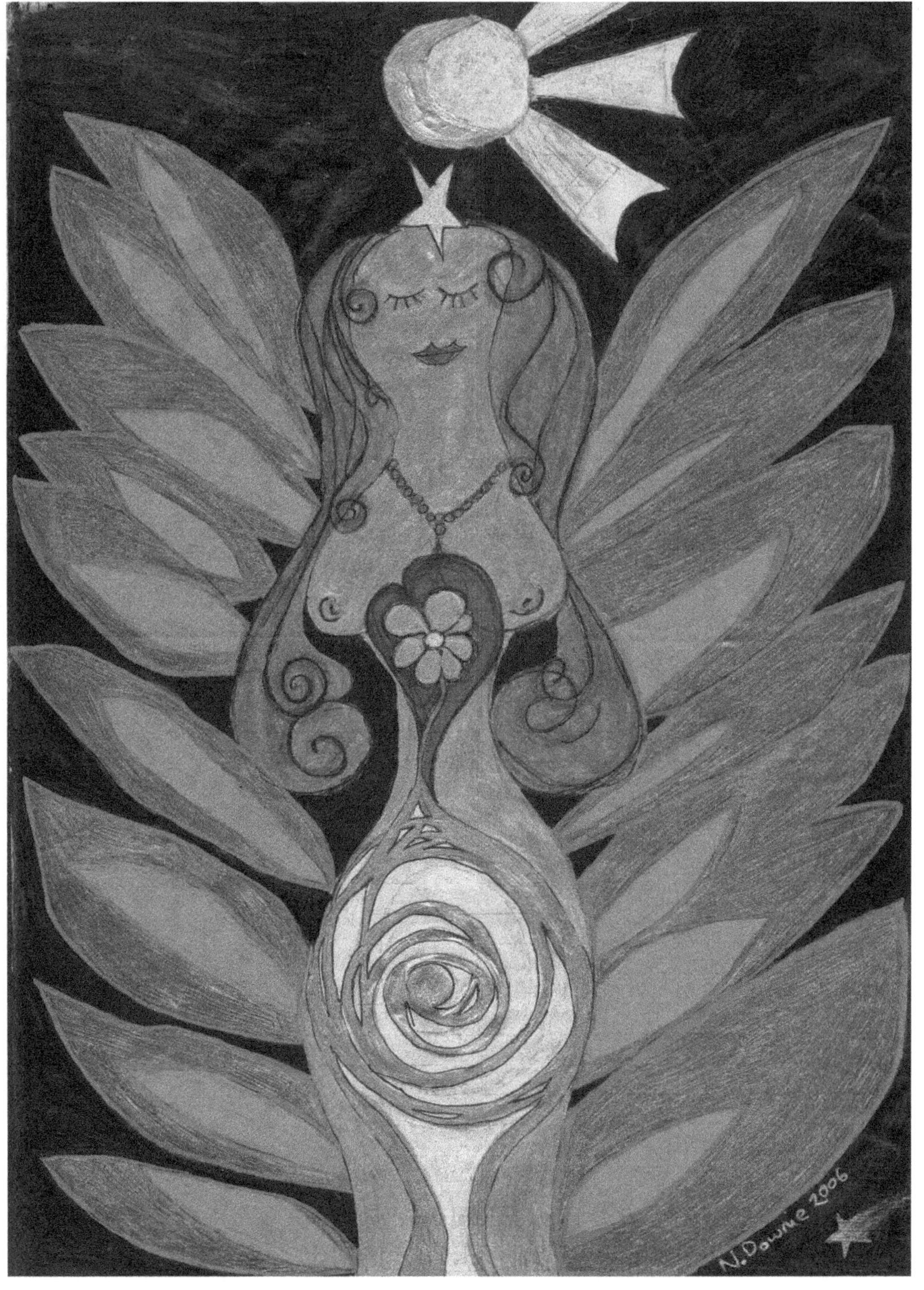

Wellbeing by Naomi

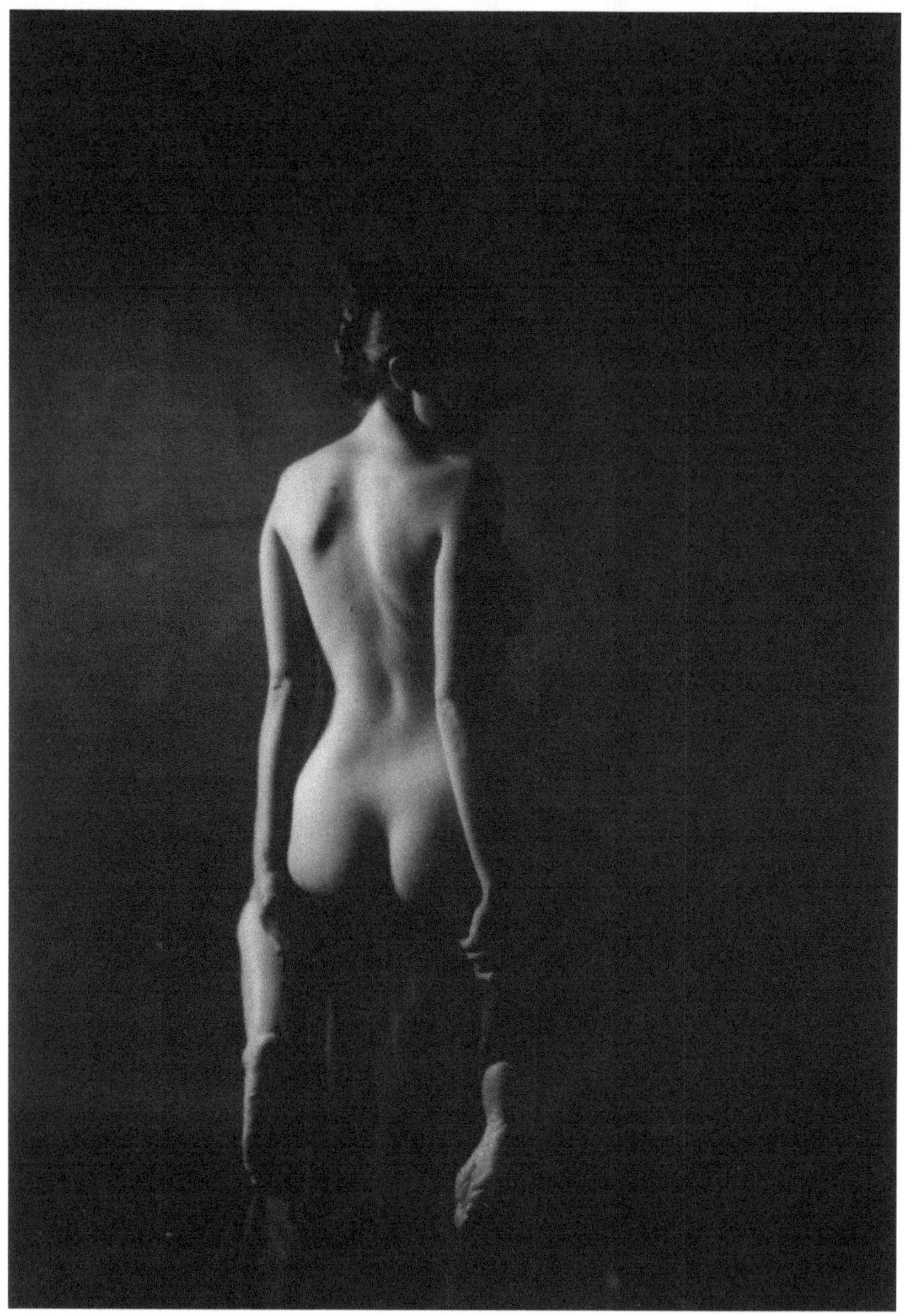

Nicole by Naomi

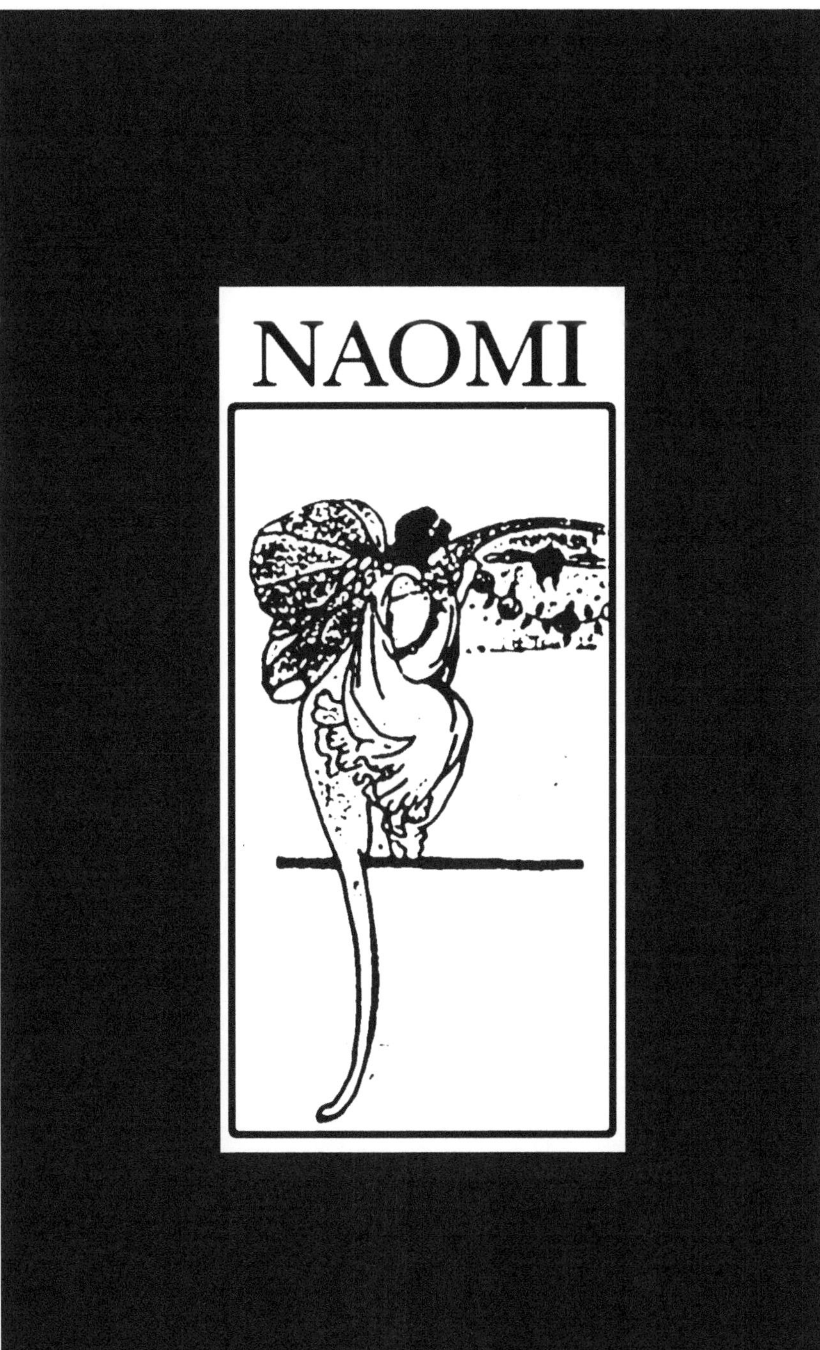
NAOMI

my beloved

your heart beats
the sound of
the mother

your strong arms
hold me safe
like the father

your body fills
my being with trust
like the brother

the light in your eyes
sparkles
like the fire of the lover

In this moment
safe in the harbour
of your arms, I sigh

you have become
my everything
my everyone

our laughter is my childhood playground
our quiet whisperings, my new philosophy

your broad shoulders, my new religious fever

your warmth now fills my blood
roaring all pathways for you

your attention luminates my cells
like the Moon at midnight
for the Sun has finally come

NAOMI

your gaze ignites my memory of divinity
this ancient wise Medusa Goddess, I am -

"I am Women", my body screams...
as it recognises the sheer
manliness of your presence

you are my Adam the first, and I am your Eve
you are my Lord Krishna and I am your Radha
I bow before you, the God within my beloved

let me be a welcoming home
a place of return
to enter and be warm

let me be a sacred cave for you
the place to feel your power
reach your Menhir of Manhood

let each entry
be a vist to my temple
a place of worship
to fill your cup
and give of yours

may our energy
our form
our mystery
Dance!

NAOMI

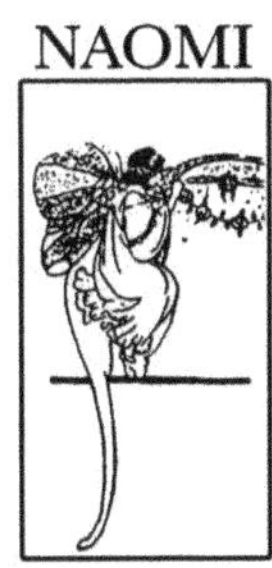

creation story

masculine life force bursting
through the feminine being
the sacred dance unfolds
Shiva and Shakti
Yin and Yang
God and Mary

rainbow serpent speeds
towards the cave of infinity
merging heaven and earth
fire and water, egg and sperm
in the frantic race of life

dream becomes form
in the waters of the mother
the mother ship calls to spirit
the breath of life
to descend like a dove

testing for health begins
both are given choice
to accept or reject, to be or not to be
this new form
this new bond
this new forever

the great witness, sacred flame
watches the Holy Grail, holy blood
nurture and feed
the germination of the seed
time of great loss, great joy!

NAOMI

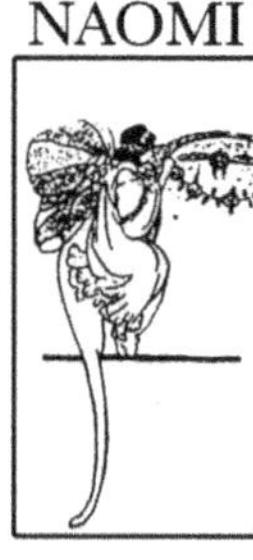

the flower blooms
woman becomes mother
mother becomes the boat
carrying her unborn child to safety
across the wide unknown ocean

I am
the journey, the boat and the witness

I will carry you surely, I will carry you safely
with my body I protect you
with my breath, I breathe for you
with all my heart, I beat life's rhythm
nourishing you with my blood

the sacred contract is activated
building potential and possibility
vows and promises
destiny and fate, weaved together
Om

Gather all the elements
earth, fire, wind, light, water, metal, sound and wood
for foundation of a physical being
cells grow divide and multiply
organs are formed
mind and heart knitted together
marrow of life and sacred structure grows

relationship between spirit mind and body
all are strongly weaved together
forming this unique tapestry of life

Flowers And Butterflies
Our Birth Into Dualities

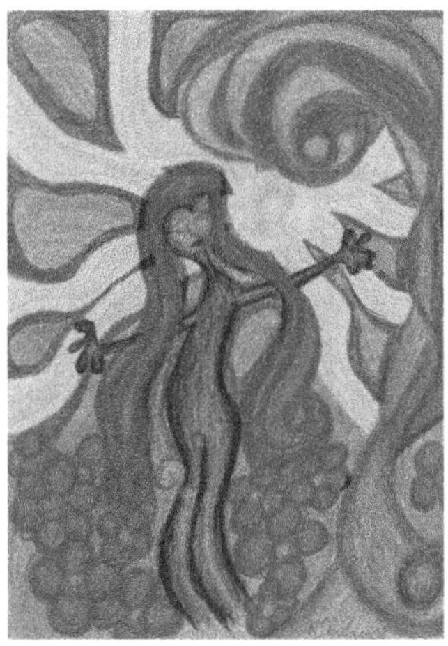

Abundance by Naomi

the goddess' embrace

I am your universe embracing your core, wrapping your night with stars, I
am the sweet nectar of woman and the soft lullaby of earth
I am Venus, Goddess of Love and a child's posy of wildflowers.

My curves are of mountains and my skin soft as a breeze
My breasts are round and ripe as full peaches ready to be tasted. Offering
a bowl of the sweet milk from the Holy Mother's nipple - nurturing your
divine connection

Join life in tenderly drinking my healthy juices
of forgiveness and return
fullness and blossoming
spirit and heart
pure and cleansed
freedom and peace
love and health

Be nourished, as I dance fire dance
burning with heat swaying my hips and waving my arms
singing, swaying, waving
tingling, shuddering and shivering with joy
as I transcend your being and enter with each breathe
touching every part of you inside, flowing in and out of you
filling your universe, embracing your heart's core
wrapping your darkness with a gown of the milky way

with my hands I hold up your sky

with my feet I deeply enter your earth
gently- I stand before you and within you
Silently whispering- I am here always, always I am here

NAOMI

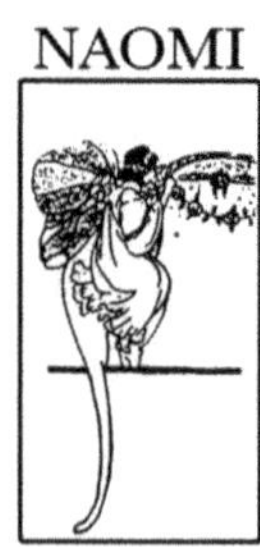

The Universal Mother

I am the life which sustains the universe
In me is the womb of all being
for I am She - The Universal Mother
I gave birth to the galaxies
I will be the one to dissolve them

I am the Blood Mother, the great womb
mother of fierce compassion

Awesome, immense, terrible
I am the mother who bled scorching blood rivers
listen to my heartbeat

Sink down to the bottom of my well
the mother who breathes for you
would kill and die for you

I am the Earth Mother, deep and rich as a field
let me nourish you with broth of chicken and barley
gentle cool breezes and warm sun on your back
a wide hipped mother like a soft feather doona
ready to cocoon you warmly inside

I am the Ocean Mother, flowing with folds of flesh
ample enough to embrace you
big enough, wide enough to hide in
to receive the burden of your pain
whispering to you

my waters are deep and wide
my sky touches infinity

Let my waves wash away your burdens
and carry them away

and carry them away
and carry them away

NAOMI

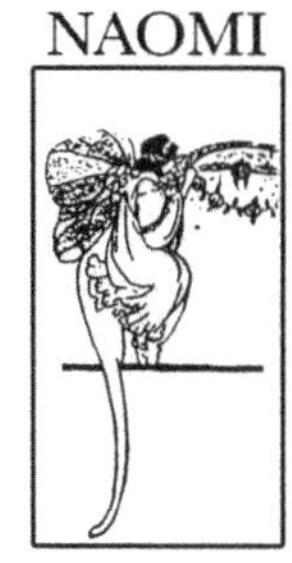

the sound of 'yes'

the moment of "yes"
the fall of "yes"
the breath of the whisper of 'yes'

power watershedding down my spine
bones unfolding awakening molding into your flesh
dancing candle flame
matching the light in your eyes
twinkling
with a fire, your fire
that burns deep

rising like a knife
poised to strike
coming in swelling
molten surges as the volcano
of long held desire
of gut animal strength
grows hard and real

the waiting is over
I sigh, as folds of clothes
fall on the floor
you lift my top
over my arms

like a mother with care
like a lover with focus
intent on the space
between us

creating the living thing
that joins two strangers
shedding day, clothes
lives, faces, places

just being here
present with you
right now, there is only you.

NAOMI

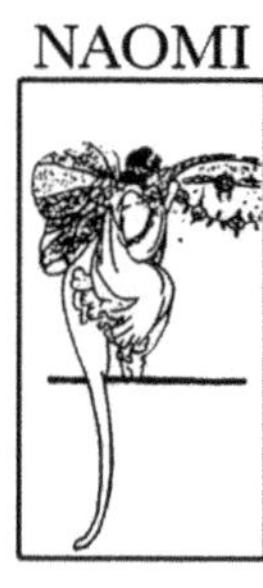

song of separation

come to me, come to me

here I am

just to be with you, be with you

is all I want

for I am longing to be with you

yearning for you, longing for you

just to be with you is all I want

lost and lonely for your breath

tired and hungry for your touch

only memories to warm my skin

warming me anew

my heart's singing you home

singing you home

let the song draw a path through time

to your ear then back home to my heart

come home

the lovers reunite

with perfumed oils and sweet water, I wash you
with honey and rose water, I wash you
my beloved, I wash you
let me take this sea sponge, scrubbing you down
nurturing every part of your body
cleaning every part of you
washing away the pain of our separation
my complete service is to you

let these tears of joy wash away your tears of sorrow
warm towels dry your hair and body
I wrap you snugly in fresh linen, to shut out the cold
offer a drink of freshly squeezed juice
revitalising you with rivers of goodness inside
here is a plate of the sweetest mango
almonds to strengthen your empty stomach
they quietly sit as he brushes her long long hair
till every part of her feels loved
the qualities of love, splendour and radiance

NAOMI

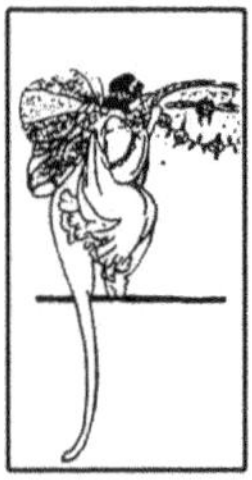

are bestowed to her, flow into her

weaved with light back into her being

renewing, replenishing all of her heart

filling hidden wells deep in her being

she sits shining with satisfaction

oysters offer up their pearls for her slender neck

a crown of stars and comets halo her hair

as she was always, the moon to him

for her dress he takes the midnight sky

wrapping it in cascading folds around her

he weaves the sunrays for a ring

plucking a star he places it on the golden orb

they watch it sparkle

her heart skips with pleasure

she takes Jupiter and places its rings around his neck

she weaves the colours of a sunset together

yellow, orange, pink and lilac

creating his golden hero's armour

NAOMI

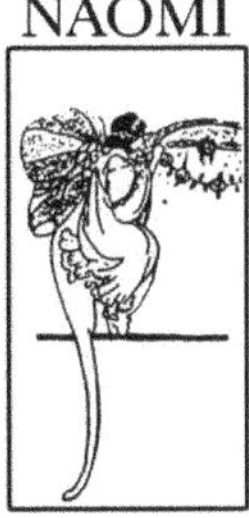

bears offer their strength and hair for his chest

lions give their roar for his warrior heart

his feet are made of mountains and his legs built from trees

his strong arms are tattooed with spiral galaxies

his sword of righteousness is formed from volcanic molten fire

his staff springs forth from the Cosmic Tree of Life

Now complete she gazes at her beloved

drinking him in, breathing him in

full of adoration and worship for her Saviour's splendour

they stand together

glittering like jewels from the earth and sky

holding her face with his beautiful hands, he speaks -

'We battled to be together, to return to the rhythm of our love, to find this place, this space, your face loving mine, all internal and external obstacles we warred and won'

As their lips touch and all matter dissolves

Into this eternal moment, embracing them with pure bliss

butterflies and doves fly, like opened petals from their feet

new rivers are formed forests grow to reach their light

the desert blooms as blessings fall from their kisses

the sky shines radiant pink with their love

Time bows down, honouring their great devotion

to each other and was still.

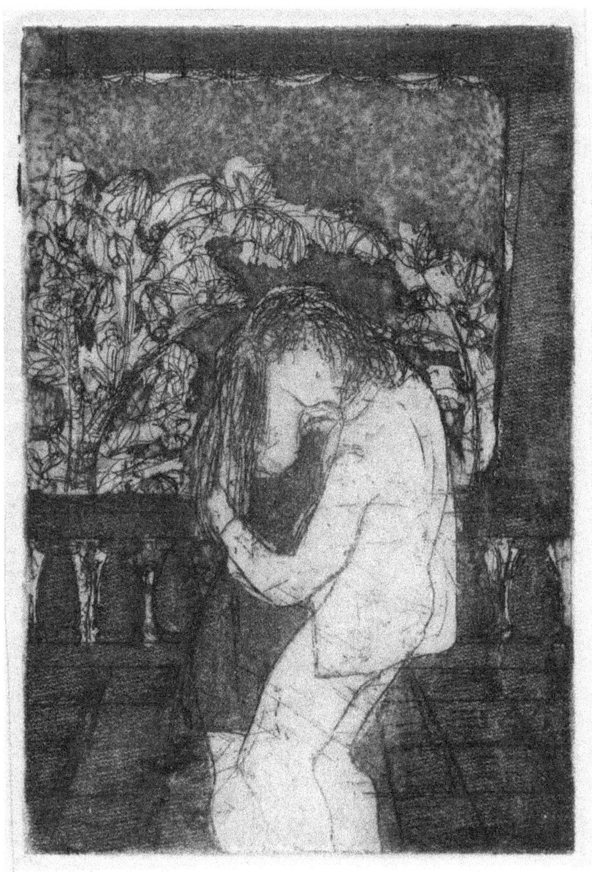

and then he kissed her with an orchestra of birds in the background
by Naomi

this kiss, this kiss, this kiss

In this kiss, a place was born
in this place, was an expanse of warm light
this light grew to surround us

a swelling and pulsing landscape
of moist and misty mountains

smooth smouldering skies
coloured in different shades of our heart's fire
glowing in our divine sight

this kiss, this kiss, ahh…this kiss
we languished in this kiss
with quietness, joy and deep satisfaction
knowing the fertile dreams we sang and nurtured into being

in this place, this kiss, our space
my soul whispers -
will you walk with me
will you breathe out my name in love
can we live inside God's heart as one?

your heart replies -
my beloved, I am drunk with joy on your nectar
and softly sing your praises

in daily acts of giving, daily acts of receiving
relishing, sharing, growing with the new

hand in hand through the old.

NAOMI

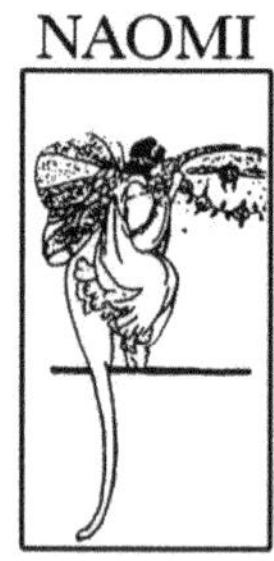

the silent work

In the quietness of my soul
a hurricane of light appears

sparkling winds of rainbows ride and glide
glittering, as they whirl the wastelands away

'Away, away', the mystic angels cry
in sweet anthem of remembrance

far from the soliloquy of insecurities
and fractured fronds of missed moments...

the self reconnects with the silence
needed to be still, in the sacred storm's eye
in this pause of peace, contentment lies

as clarity of sight awakens
to unveil crystalline landscapes of home

hundreds of lotus petals, heaven earth and sky
dreams of planets and shining ones
lighting our visions and singing
in a symphony of sound

we dance and dance
deep in the myths of the stars

NAOMI

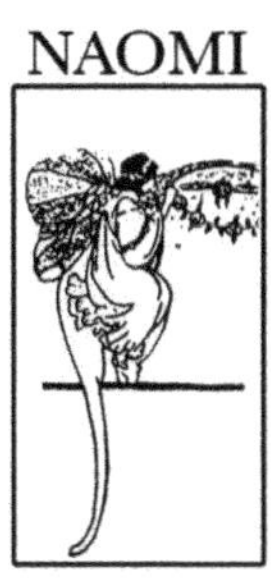

dance of prayer

stillness in movement, strength in gentleness
feel the wind touch as you move
feel the body remembering
action with awareness, communion with silence
Pause, in this moment be
the musician, mountain and maiden
then let go

let me hold your stars and touch your moon
for we are the sun
let me part any clouds that hide our light
rest awhile, as I wash off
your traveller's dust with my perfumed hair
for I am the gift of home
from my well draw deeply, your fill of living water
from my heart's fire, warm your hands and face

find your centre
with feet firmly planted
in the earth's core
stand straight and tall
point of a thousand meetings
reaching for heaven
bring up the fire energy
gather the water energy
harmonising heaven and earth

we are the materialisation of spirit
we are the bridge between heaven and earth

dance our prayer oh warrior
with the courage of the tiger
the balance of the white crane
and the beauty of the peacock
cleaning the mirror, that reflects the divine

NAOMI

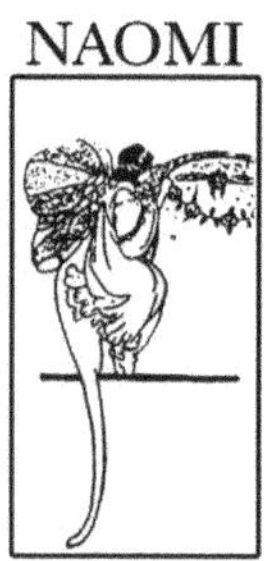

little love poem

I weave my
hearts treasures
into a robe
to wear
and share
with you

I whisper quietly
as you slowly unfold
them to reveal
my naked vulnerability

slowly I build the
courage to hold your
heart with care
and awe
in my hands

may love flow

may love flow within you, like a fountain of pure light.
may love be above you, like the sky embracing your night.
may love be beneath you, like the earth strengthening your bones.
may love be on your left and right side, like the wings of angels and doves.
may love be in front of you, like a lamp guiding you home.
may love be behind you, like the wind encouraging you on
may love be between us, like rainbows bridging the way to our heart.
may love be our communion, like the petals of a rose all join as one
in our centre
because then my beloved,
then we will all blossom
offering our sweet perfume to the Sun

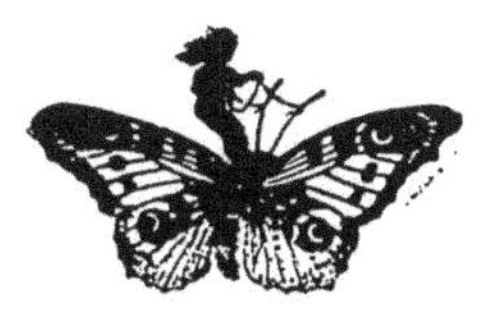

I am striving to give the Divine in myself

to the Divine in All.

Porphyry

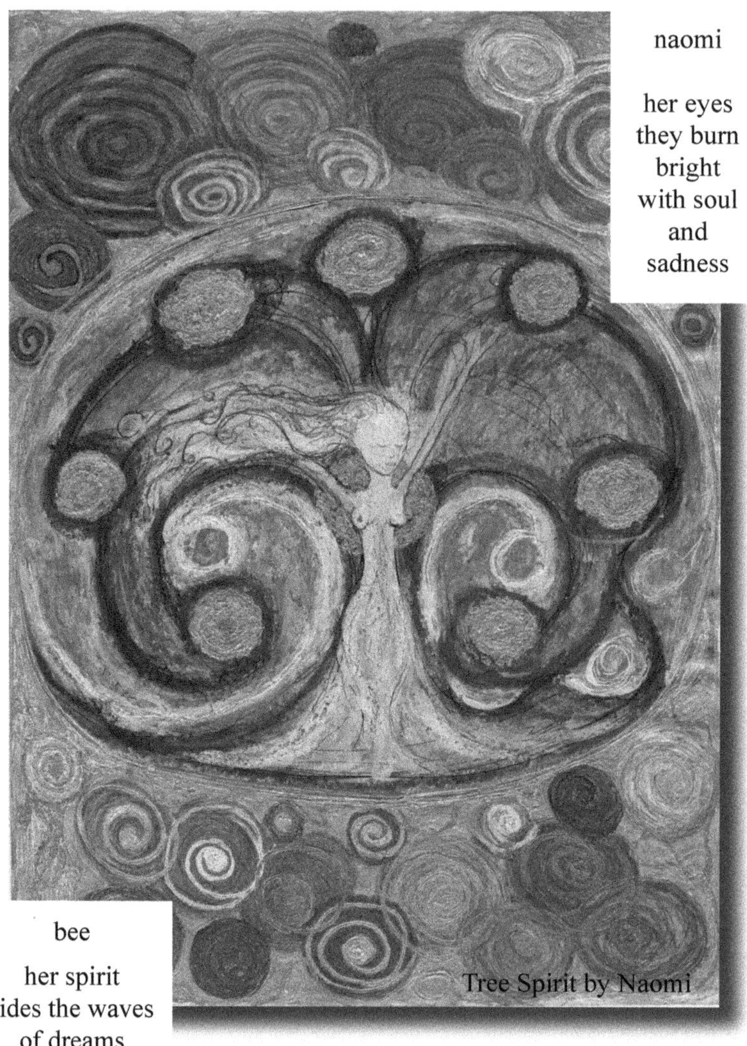

Tree Spirit by Naomi

naomi

her eyes
they burn
bright
with soul
and
sadness

bee

her spirit
rides the waves
of dreams
her soul holds
the hand of
the moon

the mad man, the lover, and the poet,

all have ways of knowing

Shakespeare

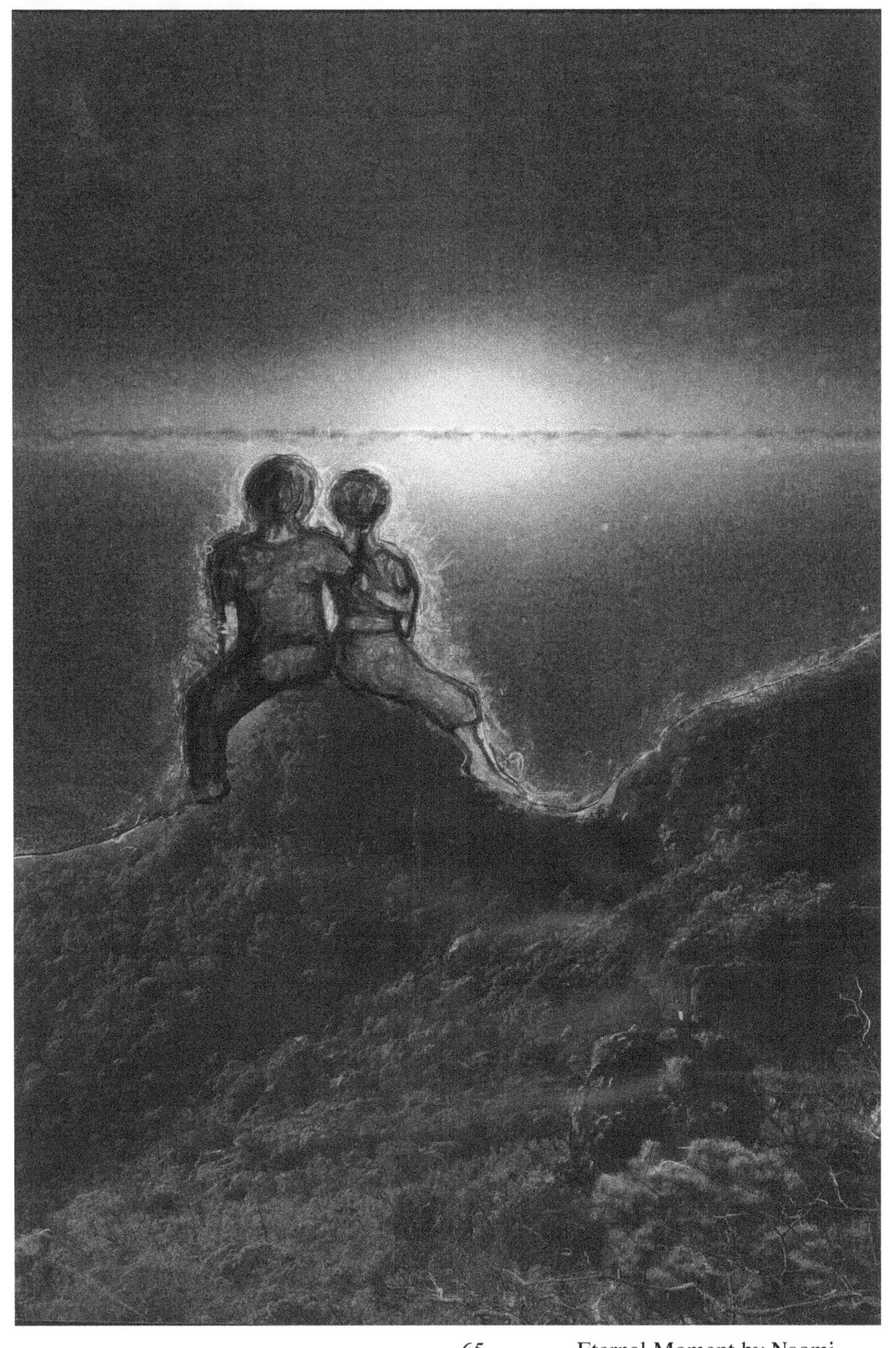

Eternal Moment by Naomi

www.ingramcontent.com/pod-product-compliance
Lightning Source LLC
LaVergne TN
LVHW052357100826
845147LV00013B/859
* 9 7 8 0 6 4 6 5 0 7 7 6 7 *